G000153329

# Wildness

*Voices of the Sacred Landscape*

# Wildness

*Voices of the Sacred Landscape*

An Anthology Featuring:
Gunilla Norris
Jason Kirkey
Theodore Richards
Walker Abel
Amy Nawrocki
Eric D. Lehman
David K. Leff
Gary Whited
Andrew Jarvis
Francesca G. Varela
Iris Graville
James Scott Smith
Diane P. Freedman
Mary Petiet
Audrey Henderson
William Henry Searle
Linda Flaherty Haltmaier
Gail Steeves Collins-Ranadive
Edited by L. M. Browning

### Homebound Publications
*Ensuring that the mainstream isn't the only stream.*

Printed in the United States of America
as well as the United Kingdom and Australia.

Paperback ISBN 978-1-938846-71-7
Front Cover Image © Alberto Restifo
Cover and Interior Designed by Leslie M. Browning

*www.homeboundpublications.com*

10 9 8 7 6 5 4 3 2 1

Homebound Publications greatly values the natural
environment and invests in environmental conservation.
Our books are printed on paper with chain of custody
certification from the Forest Stewardship Council,
Sustainable Forestry Initiative, and the Program for
the Endorsement of Forest Certification. In addition, each year
Homebound Publications donates 1% of our net profit to a
humanitarian or ecological charity.

IN CELEBRATION OF HOMEBOUND PUBLICATIONS' 5TH ANNIVERSARY

Dedicated in gratitude to
our readers, authors, staff, and unnamed benefactors.

---

# Contents

About the Press

*I only went out for a walk and finally concluded to stay out*
*'till sundown, for going out, I found, was really going in.*
—JOHN MUIR

Theodore Richards is the director and founder of The Chicago Wisdom Project and the author of several books. He is the recipient of numerous literary awards, including two Independent Publisher Awards and the Nautilus Book Award. He lives in Chicago with his wife and daughters.

www.theodorerichards.com.

# The Three Skies

## by Theodore Richards

*All skies, like the stars themselves, are memories, existing*
*simultaneously here and elsewhere, at once in this moment,*
*in the eyes that take them in, and also in unfathomable*
*depths of the fullness of time.*

## I.

I ARRIVED ON A LATE SUMMER DAY IN THE BERKSHIRES, alone and uncertain, a young man who didn't even know who he was. I'd spent my entire, brief life in cities, contemplating words and justice and other things that human beings do. I had been a Gilgamesh, building walls in the Uruk of my human mind.

Now I found myself on the side of a mountain, smoking bidis and wondering what had driven me to spend the next four months in the middle of nowhere. I was seeking to find my own Enkidu. To become wild again.

The Berkshires, like the rest of the Appalachians, are old mountains, their once-jagged peaks worn away by millennia of winds. Their gentle slopes are ideal for wandering and hiking. But these are rocky soils, less than ideal for farming. The first Europeans who came to them were filled with a belief that the soils could be tamed through their Protestant Work Ethic, their belief in their dominion over nature. Now, as I wandered through the forests, I found the fences those farmers had once made, in fields that had returned, in the blink of an eye, to forest. They, like Gilgamesh, had had to realize the hard way that their walls were mere hubris and vanity.

I did begin to feel, to remember, some of my own wildness. I sat out upon the edge of the mountain, looking across the forest, watching the dusk descend. And as Autumn came, I wandered through the deep and mysterious forest, surrounded by exploding colors of floating leaves. I could feel the texture of the living earth in ways I never had before. I smelled the rotting leaves as they returned to soil.

And then, each night, I looked up. From millions of miles away, and from millions of years ago, the deepest darkness of night exploded in my own eyes. I saw those stars and remembered, just a little, who I was.

## II.

I LEFT THE MOUNTAINS AND WENT TO AFRICA. In the tropics, dusk is over in the blink of an eye; stars pulsate rapidly from periwinkle sky to human eye like seeds of matter rising up from the quantum foam. As old as Africa is for the human, those stars were immeasurably older.

I lived on a dairy farm in eastern Zimbabwe, many miles from a telephone. Few had electricity in the area in which I lived. My job was to teach literacy to women. So most of my days were spent walking from village to village to meet with students. We crossed streams on bridges made of fallen tree limbs, ate mangos plucked from trees.

After long and tiring days, I retired to our little house overlooking the broad savannah valley. And I watched the stars.

There is no older place in the human imagination than Africa. Our long legs were shaped by those savannahs; the leopards that roamed them and hid stealthily in the Baobabs shaped our minds and our communities. There, we learned to be wanderers. We learned to care for each other in community, because it was the only way to survive.

And of course, in the darkness each night in our journeys, we looked up. Star and human eye came together to produce that most human of offspring: The Story.

I felt the pull of the road. I needed to move, to wander. I left the farm and headed east, over the mountains and into Mozambique.

At the time—this was the mid-nineties—Mozambique was poorest country on the planet. Only recently its decades long civil war had ended, leaving a country with little infrastructure. Its unnamed roads were pock-marked from neglect and the bombs brought from the West.

I arrived in Beira, a city by the sea, and was accosted by a hoard of people. It felt as if no one had visited in decades. Land-mine victims hopped up to me, begging—I understood little Portuguese but their pleas were clear. Two men hurried me into a taxi, a car that required the second man to run along side, pushing while the car started up. He jumped in the moving car and we drove out of the city center, along the coast, past mighty and decaying shipwrecks along the beach, past boys playing football and fishermen singing work songs.

I spent week on the beach, in a tent next to a beach bar. I ate coconuts and listened to the surf. There, for the first time, I began to write stories. In this post-apocalyptic scene, a memory of the past came to me, of a life in which the brightest lights were not obscured by artificial ones. I saw the stars and began to tell stories, like my ancestors.

## III.

THE WANDERING SPIRIT TOOK HOLD OF ME AGAIN a couple
of years later. I crossed the Asian continent, finding myself
in the Middle Eastern deserts of southern Jordan.

I had visited the great, ancient and abandoned city of Petra,
where, completely emptied of tourists—they'd been scared off by
another Palestinian uprising on the other side of the Jordan—I
could wander and play in ruins. I caught a lonely bus south to the
desert stop of Wadi Rum.

Not far at all from Wadi Rum, the Israelites had wandered, millennia ago. Deuteronomy 26:5 proclaims that the ancestor of the
Israelites was a "wandering Aramean." This memory of our wandering roots, Aramean or not, resides in us all. For most of human
history, we were wanderers. This is a memory we carry in the very
structure of our bodies, not to mention our wandering souls.

We also carry the memory of darkness. The bright lights of
Modernity—the En*light*enment—have suppressed the darkness
in our selves and in our sterile, urban and suburban lives. As a
result, one must travel far to see the brightest lights.

In the desert, land and sky are as open and vast as the
imagination. There is room there, in the emptiness, for the human
to bring forth new stories, new worlds. I wandered among the
cliffs and dunes for hours, day after day, resting in the shade when
the Sun's power became too great.

The desert reminds us that we can stop, too, even as wanderers.
It reminds us that Earth and Sun, not the human need for produc-
tivity and busy-ness, are better guides for our quotidian patterns.

At night, the desert stars filled me with an emptiness as
profound as the desert itself. I sat and watched, tearfully, as I saw,
in them, an ancestral story, a story of where we all come from. The

stardust. The stories told by the fire. The wandering Aramean. Modernity has filled our lives with so many things, so many distractions. So many bright lights.

But the brightest lights are only brought forth in the vast and empty darkness.

Iris Graville writes creative nonfiction from her home on Lopez Island, WA. She holds an MFA in writing from the Northwest Institute of Literary Arts and is the publisher of *Shark Reef* Literary Magazine. Her first book, *Hands at Work*, received several accolades, including a Nautilus Book Award. "Boris' Bluff," past winner of the Oregon Quarterly Northwest Perspectives Essay Contest, figures prominently in Iris's memoir, *Hiking Naked: A Quaker Woman's Search for Balance*, forthcoming from Homebound Publications in 2017.

www.irisgraville.com

# Boris' Bluff

## by Iris Graville

Boris' Bluff. You won't find it in hiking guidebooks or on topographical maps. Guides don't take visitors there, either; tourists wouldn't be impressed by this rock outcropping, a twenty-minute wander from our home the two years we lived in the isolated village of Stehekin, Washington. But Boris' Bluff awed me.

It was Boris, our tabby cat, who first led me there. It's not so much a bluff as the alliterative name we gave it suggests, but more like an over-sized, moss-flecked pitcher's mound. Just beyond the sloping rock, cottonwoods and pines start their ascent to the foothills and peaks surrounding it. If not for the slice of sky visible through the canopy, you could believe the world ends right there.

Stehekin, translated as "the way through," was named by Skagit and Salish tribes migrating between the east and west sides of Washington State. My husband and I and our two kids vacationed there regularly over the course of ten years. We'd arrive on a passenger-only ferry that navigates once daily up fifty-five-mile-long Lake Chelan. Highways were blasted through a stretch of the rocky lakeshore, but none ever made it all the way to Stehekin and its cliffed shoreline. Telephone lines never got there either, and the mountains shooting up from the valley floor block cell phone transmission.

Long before our move to Stehekin, vacations there schooled us in the way of life in this village of eighty-five, fringed by North Cascades National Park. We practiced Stehekin-style grocery shopping—mail your list and blank check to the Safeway store at the other end of the lake; pick up your groceries at the boat three days later. We outwitted biting black flies and temperatures in the upper 90s by skinny-dipping in the icy Stehekin River. On a stay during a winter holiday, we woke to three feet of fresh snow, read by kerosene lamp when the hydroelectric power went down, and inched a vintage pick-up along single-lane, ice-crusted village roads.

Early on in our visits, hikes into Stehekin's backcountry renewed my zeal for my work as a public health nurse. As the years went on, though, my fire for promoting health for the poor and underserved began to sputter; trekking the mountains no longer re-ignited me. I dreaded yet another referral for a pregnant teen, or sitting again in a cigarette-smoke-infused apartment teaching a harried mom alternatives to yelling at her toddler to shut up. I couldn't face more refugees who had forgotten to take their tuberculosis medications, or hear once more from supervisors that we had to increase visit numbers. It all weighed on me like an overstuffed backpack, its straps digging into my shoulders and its heft pounding my lower back. I began to question if nursing, the work I had felt called to, was what I was still meant to do.

Finally, one year, instead of vacationing in Stehekin, my family and I moved there. They wanted adventure. I sought escape. Hoped for my own "way through." That first fall and winter, I filled two journals with run-on sentences of complaint, criticism of myself and others, questioning of my values, and fear. I didn't realize I was writing the textbook on burnout. By the time most of the snow melted, I had only questions. Had I failed? Or was I being nudged to different work?

One spring day, Boris and I again tramped to the bluff. He coiled beside me as I sat on the sun-warmed stone, his purr vibrating in the windless air. I breathed in Ponderosa pines and Douglas firs. Reaching a hundred feet upward, their long history preceded me. At the base of their trunks, saplings signaled new growth. Snowy peaks towered five thousand feet above, their ridges cascading in ripples of purple beyond my vision. Unexpectedly, I sensed that Boris and I weren't alone. The cement block of worry about the sick immigrants and the struggling teen mothers lifted from my back. Tears welled as I grasped that I have my part to play, but it's not up to me alone. On Boris' Bluff, I embraced both my smallness and my greatness.

I don't live in Stehekin anymore, but it lives in me. Boris died last year. I didn't go back to the old house, or the old job. My family and I moved to a community on a rural island in Puget Sound. Here, I balance work as a school nurse with writing. I'm seeking still—not escape, but attention to God's presence. So here, I climb the saltwater-lashed cliffs of Iceberg Point and sit among firs, their wind-twisted trunks bent toward the ground. I imagine the Coast Salish of the past, fishing for salmon and gathering gin-scented juniper berries on that "way through" the Cascades, perhaps pausing awhile at Boris' Bluff.

L.M. Browning is an award-winning author of nine books. In her writing, Browning explores the confluence of the natural landscape and the interior landscape. In 2010, Leslie debuted with a three-title contemplative poetry series. These three books went on to garner several accolades including a total of 3 pushcart-prize nominations, the Nautilus Gold Medal for Poetry and *Forward Reviews'* Book of the Year Award. Balancing her passion for writing with her love of learning, Browning sits on the Board of Directors for the Independent Book Publishers' Association. She is a graduate of the University of London and a Fellow with the International League of Conservation Writers. She is partner at Hiraeth Press as well as Founder and Editor-in-Chief of *The Wayfarer.* In 2011, Browning opened Homebound Publications. She is currently working to complete a B.A. at Harvard University's Extension School in Cambridge, Massachusetts.

www.lmbrowning.com

# Altruistic Hiking

by L.M. Browning

May 4, 2015 | Napatree Point, Rhode Island

THE FIRST TRUE WARMTH OF SPRING ARRIVES and Alex and I decide to drive down to Watch Hill, Rhode Island and walk Napatree Point, a tucked away strip of shore in southern Rhode Island.

It is said that the name "Napatree" is derived from Nape (Neck) of Trees. Up until the Great September Gale of 1815, the land was densely wooded. The trees were stripped away by the storm, the strength of which would rate a category 3 on the modern Saffir-Simpson Hurricane Scale.

My fond memories of Napatree go back some 30 years to when my mother first brought me to walk the beach as a child. After strolling along the shore, we would walk into the nearby town of Watch Hill (a small endearing beach village with a Hamptons-esque quality) where she would give me a couple dollars to ride the carousel, which lies at the heart of the village.

The "Flying Horses Carousel" as it is called, is composed of 20 horses, suspended by chains underneath a multicolored canopy. When the carousel spins, centrifugal force pulls the horses outward, thus it earned its name the "Flying Horses". The jolly tune that plays while the horses fly emanates from a hand-crank organ found at the center of the main pillar. In 1987, the carousel was declared a National Historical Landmark. It has run in the village of Watch Hill since 1879 when a traveling carnival was forced to leave it behind.

I still remember gripping the chains as I sat on the horses, the leather strap holding me to the hard saddle straining against my waist as I reached for the brass ring.

On this particular spring afternoon, Alex and I pass through Watch Hill on our way to Napatree. I see the carousel spinning like a dervish, the chimes and pipes of the organ music are still just as enchanting as when I first heard them. I pause for a moment at the rail and watch the jubilant colors turn, the laughter of the children a joyful counterpoint to music. As we stand there, I wonder how I was ever small enough to fit on one of the ponies, and, with a scent of popcorn, candy, and ice cream in the air, we press on to the point.

This day hike was to be the first since the fall. In the summer of 2014 I suffered a *Trimalleolar* fracture and dislocation. (In layman's terms: I dislocated my ankle and broke it in three places. More damaging than the bone breaks, was the extensive soft tissue damage done by the dislocation.) All of this resulting in what is termed an "unstable ankle fracture" that can only be mended through surgical intervention.

If this injury had happened 100 years sooner, I'd never walked properly again and most certainly would have re-broken it several times within my life, but, in this day and age, titanium heals all. Run enough screws, plates, and wire through the bone and even the most broken of joints can be held together.

Confined to my bed for six weeks after the reconstructive surgery, I went from hiking through the woodlands of New England to shuffling along on a brand new walker—fully outfitted with four spiffy tennis balls. Six months recovery, three months of physical therapy, four different casts, and two braces later, I find myself moving along better each day.

Napatree would be the test of the still-healing joint. I exchanged the walnut cane for a metal trek pole, strung my shoes together, threw them over my shoulder, and set out towards the beach. The first hurdle would be the rather tall sand dune that one must climb to reach the sheltered shore. This posed a problem for my ankle, which still had difficulty reaching certain angles.

"The tall sand is particularly difficult," I comment to Alex as we start the climb, "you don't realize the dozens of corrections the muscles and ligaments in your ankle makes to support you in the uneven sand until you can feel every single tendon firing and straining."

My foot could strain to reach a 90 degree position, but pushing off from that angle to take the next step was terribly uncomfortable. Determined as I was to see the ocean, I shuffled up the dune and gently walked down the other side, descending to the shore, a long rock jetty at my left and the sandy peninsula of the shore stretching out, making my way down to the compacted sand along the waterline.

We started down the shore. Pushed by the high gales, the waves drove hard against the shore. Black Back gulls hovered like feathered dirigibles overhead, perching expertly on the turbulent wind. Only moments before, they'd had their morning feast. Opened mussels and scooped out spider crab heads were scattered along the sand. Every now and again we came upon a lone blue mussel sitting upon the sand that had managed to survive the feeding frenzy. I picked up each one, aware of the little frightened creature closed tight within, and tossed it into the salty swells.

All along the rock jetty erected to shelter Watch Hill, cluster mussels grew as thick as dragon scales. Somehow, I'd never noticed the colony until now. I followed the wall of rocks into the cold May waters of the North Atlantic. A species of sea lettuce

clung in-between the shells, the translucent topical green inter-
spersed among the black and blue mussels. Something about the
densely huddled mussels made me think about community and
the joy of growing together.

Soothed by the surf and fresh wind, I made the decision (perhaps foolishly) to walk the full length of the beach, walk all the
way do to the fort.

In addition to the present-day nature conservancy, Napatree
Point was also home to Fort Mansfield. In 1883, a joint Army-
Navy Board that would later be known as the "Endicott Board"
issued a report exposing the defenselessness of the United States'
coast. Fort Mansfield was but one of the 53 shoreline forts
constructed along the East coast during the Endicott Period
(1890-1910) in an effort to secure coastal towns and harbors
from attack. 81 installations were constructed in total. In 1898,
the government purchased 60 acres along Napatree Point and
construction for Fort Mansfield began. The facility was completed
in 1902 and acted as a small, single company, outpost. In July 1907
during routine war games a fatal flaw was discovered in outpost,
which led to the deactivation of the fort in 1909. Ten years later,
the fort was demolished; only 3 concrete gun placements were left
behind. Remnants of two still remain, while one has become a
victim to rising tides and sea erosion, which has pushed the beach
back some 200 feet since 1898.

Almost immediately after deciding to walk down to the fort,
the smooth path grew difficult. Mounds of dense stone littered
the shore. The gravel, while smoothed by the tumbling tide, was
rough against by bare feet that had been softened over my months
of inactivity. A fierce tide must have deposited gritty sand up
along the shore. A strip of red kelp pushed up by the waves drew
a line from the dunes down along the length of the beach off into

the distance. It had dried in the sun and now waited to be folded back into the sea during the next high tide. Intermingled within the leaves, were a confetti of crustaceans and mollusks: tiny sea urchins, clams, mussels, and sea slippers stacked one on top of the next (some alive, some dead).

Alex and I always hike altruistically, routinely picking up clumps of still-closed blue mussels and stacked sea slipper stranded high on the beach and tossing them back into the water. Some creatures were sadly beyond aid. Dismembered legs and heads of spider crabs, shrimp, Atlantic blue crabs, rock crabs, lobsters, and horseshoe crabs trailed along the shore. The brown sand dotted now and again by the ripped sacks of the devil purses—the eggs sacks of sharks, skates, and chimaeras (most likely skates in this case).

Two thirds of the way down the shore, we spotted a lone survivor. I'd found a small graveyard of horseshoe crab skeletons. The waters around Napatree are a mating ground for pre-historic creatures. (The earliest evidence of the species dating back some 450 million years, to the Ordovician period.) I hovered over one of the dead. It was intact. It lay on its back legs and tail stiffly pointed in the air. "Poor crab." I commented empathetically. Alex came closer to see what exactly I'd found when suddenly the crab's legs started flailing rapidly in the air. I lean in closer to see what was going on, noticing that the crab had been hogtied—tail in all—by a long piece of red kelp. Black back gulls started circling overhead, likewise drawn by the crab's movement. Rushing to the crab's aid, Alex carried him (judging by the small size, it was most likely male) back down to the surf where he floated down into the obscured depths of the ocean floor. We walked on.

The talk of the insignificant stresses of the business day fell silent. Both of us basking in the knowledge that something of value had been accomplished today: We'd saved a life. (And not just one life actually but dozens.) You see, while few know it, I am the patron of sea slippers. While walking Napatree, every few yards I inevitably find a stack of the tiny creatures drying out far up on the shore that I must stop rescue. Something about the smallness of their little community and their fragility compels me to help them.

Sea slippers are prominent along the shores of Napatree so our hike is more a rescue mission than an outing. A type of sea snail, sea slippers are also known as common Atlantic slipper snails, quarterdeck shells, or Atlantic Slipper Limpets. Often sea slippers will cling on to rocks, pilings or even horseshoe crabs but most often they live in stacks. The oldest female being the base of the pile while the younger small males are on top, the species is a sequential hermaphrodite. If the female should die, the largest male in the stack will become female.

As we walked on and I ferry the stranded creatures back to the sea, I thought back to the sometimes-absurd lengths I'd gone to over the years to help animals; whether it was when I was eight and I cared for a lone killdeer chick after its mother died, to the time when I was learning how to drive on the dirt roads of rural upstate New York when I suddenly swerved inexplicably.

"What happened?" the instructor exclaimed at a loss.

"Woolly bear" I replied meekly, "there was a woolly bear in the road. It wasn't like there was oncoming traffic." I went on, trying to expel the dumbfounded look creasing his face. We came to a stop along the utterly deserted country road.

He quickly looked out the back window , "How did you even see it?"

"I was looking." I replied, not knowing what else to say.

*        *        *

For as long as I can remember, I've felt an overflowing empathy for wildlife. I feel more connected to the encroached upon animal than I do that of Western society. The kinship I feel for the wild has been there within me since I was a child. I spent the summers of my childhood knee-deep in ponds meeting bullfrogs and sun turtles, and my springs and autumns exploring the woodlands around our home. I can't pinpoint exactly what, but something about the exchange when I encounter an animal in the wild is revelatory to me. After each encounter, I am left feeling varying depths of awe, and in this awe find peace and belonging.

Nature is a mystery of immeasurable complexity that cannot and need not be fully understood. The sense of awe we feel when beholding the wild is rooted in our appreciation of the infinite intricacy interweaving all things together, and the unspoken surrender of our need to comprehend it all. Awe arises as the ego recedes. It is an instant wherein we recognize the magnitude of elements at work, and are grateful for having even the smallest of roles in the drama of existence playing out within the universe.

Looking up from my ponderings, I see Alex climbing through a labyrinth of rocks scattered within the waves. We'd made it to the fort. As Alex explored the surround, I sat on a cluster of rocks for a time. The hollow iron bell of a buoy clanged in time with the swells in the distance. Stepping from rock to rock, I moved deeper out into the water, finally coming to rest on a larger boulder only half submerged in the incoming tide. Looking down at my feet in the cold water I witnessed a plethora of life. Blue mussels, slipper shells, and a fleet of sea snails no bigger than pebbles swarmed in the pooling breakwater. A tiny spider crab reached a claw out from under a nearby rock. A dead one lay only a few inches away. Hopefully not a companion.

A garden of barnacles covered the side of each rock. Some were so large the pearl petals of the calcareous plates were clearly visible. I glanced back at the mile and a half of beach we'd covered. As my foot ached, a single thought occurred to me: We still have to walk back.

A flood of worry entered me, but I pushed the worry from my mind. That journey would be confronted later. The moment, I reminded myself, wasn't for dwelling on the difficulties that lay ahead, but appreciating the beauty already present.

Isak Dinesen famously writes, "The cure for anything is salt water: sweat, tears or the sea." As the snowy spray from the breaking waves kisses my face, this truth resounds. Setting out this morning, my mind was heavy from work and worry, my body weary from illness and injury. Yet the sea, with its consoling balm, had washed that strain away, even if only for a time. In the distance, I heard scream a pair of ospreys. A flock of four oystercatchers chattered loudly as they beat their wings across the horizon. Piping Plovers scuttled about almost indistinguishable from the dried grass speckling the dunes. The bell sounded. My bare scarred leg soaked in the cold salty Atlantic. The waves crash upon the ruined battlements of the fort. The wind suddenly shifted, leaving my mind to soak in the stillness.

Gunilla Norris' parents were world travelers in the Swedish diplomatic corps and so she grew up essentially in three places—Argentina, Sweden and the United States. As a child she was given a rich exposure to different languages and cultures. She received her B.A. from Sarah Lawrence College and her M.S. from Bridgeport University in the field of human development. She is a mother and a grandmother. She has been a psychotherapist in private practice for more than thirty years and has felt privileged to accompany many people on their journeys to growth and healing. Her special love has been teaching meditation and leading contemplative workshops of many kinds. As a writer Gunilla has published eleven children's books, two books of poetry, the latest, *Joy is the Thinnest Layer*, was published by Homebound Publications. She is best known for her eight books on spirituality: *Being Home, Becoming Bread, Inviting Silence, A Mystic Garden, Simple Ways, Sheltered in the Heart, Match* and *Embracing the Seasons.*

www.gunillanorris.com

# Our Place in the Wonder

## A Poetic Offering by Gunilla Norris

IN THESE POEMS I AM EXPLORING THE LINK between a felt state of being and an aspect of the natural world. I am a walking, talking, feeling human being and a peony, a tree, an owl as well as a feral cat on the prowl. For me to explore in writing how I belong in wonder, in imagination and in nature is to learn to live in a more grounded way. The gaps I feel between me and the subjects of my poems diminish. Don't all things somehow interpenetrate? Can't the feel of the whole be sensed in the smallest of details? I believe so.

## Under the Maple

with its dark red leaves,
my back to the constancy
of the gnarled trunk, I am
saying goodbye to things
I know best: summer,
the sky so impossibly blue,
and the October sun, golden
on my skin. This time I feel
how my sap is drawn down
to roots, to stillness and
something that can't be named.

Below, the seasons are gone,
no perceivable sunshine, but
it is in that darkness I can be
made light again—a human loam
so friable it allows death,
the cracked casing,
the beginning. I want to trust
that a maple sprouts, or
a woman does, roots digging down,
stem pushing up. Soon,
soon she'll leaf out.

# With a Cane

Today
　　I begin
　　　　walking.
My eyes don't see the ground
as well as they used to.
My feet in their modern maturity shoes
still wobble where
the going is uneven.

This time
　　of growing older
　　　　　　and in need
of staking, of keeping upright somehow
despite the pull of age and gravity,
wants that little tap that the tip of the cane makes
when it strikes home.
Not yet the sound of a clump,

but a kind of
　　syncopation
　　　　　as I walk out
to stake the peonies heavy with buds.
Am I, too, being staked
for blooming—like a white creamy flower
that dissolves in a moment of heavy rain
that is sure to come?

How strange
    to be filled
        with surrender.
Held by twine and sticks, the stalks
will be left without flowers, but
still green, I can feel how urgent it is
to continue to garden my life,
to be unfinished.
Today
   I begin again
      walking...

# One-ing

It's like this—
my body wants to pray
if I would just let it.
It's hard to let it.
But in the end
it turns out to be
like silencing a radio.

The endless lists lie down
on the table,
white scraps of paper
helter skelter.
They look better scattered
than stacked neatly
on a clip board.

The dirty dishes stick together
in the sink and are content
waiting for a human hand.
The sofa cushions regain their loft
when I stand, and I do stand up
for this and for
the inner music beginning

without sound. It rushes
through my legs and out
the tips of my fingers.

It moves me.
Directly my feet fall in love
with the wooden floor
and glide with no hesitation.

My trunk sways...I am
a tree, a river, Spring rain,
maybe a heron ruffling its wings,
an owl, a feral cat on the prowl.
I am. I am.
What other name could be better?
What other name does anyone have?

For Gail Collins-Ranadive, writing has always been the best way to stay centered and make sense of life's experiences, then share it. Sometimes this brings forth books, such as when visiting with in-laws in India and tutoring on the Hopi Mesa birthed picture books for children. Her MFA produced *Finding the Voice Inside*, a book of writing exercises for women. Years of writing sermons resulted in *Light Year, A Seasonal Primer for Spiritual Focus*. Her interim ministry migrations became *Nature's Calling*, and retirement in Las Vegas inspired *Chewing Sand*, both Homebound Publications books. This piece comes from her sabbatical book: *Inner Canyon, Where Deep Time Meets Sacred Space*. Currently, she and her partner are involved in the climate movement, both in Las Vegas where they winter and in Denver during the summer. The working title of that unfolding manuscript is *Dinosaur Dreaming*.

# Bright Angels at the River

## by Gail Collins-Ranadive

IT WAS COLD, OVERCAST, THREATENING RAIN AND SNOW as I gathered up my gear and walked over to the stone mule corral for orientation. My part time sabbatical year on the South Rim of the Grand Canyon was half over, and I was finally about to make it down to the River. But instead of hiking, I'd ride the mule train.

Orientation was both amusing and intimidating, with the emphasis on making us realize this is not a Disneyland adventure that is predictable and controllable: these were real animals with minds of their own…we're to treat them like substitute teachers reigning in fourth graders who have been at recess for a month, the month the trail had been closed and these mules have spent eating and doing whatever else mules do when they're not working.

There were three strings of mules for three groups of riders. The first two groups were taken into the corral and matched with mules…they were going down as far as Indian Garden and Plateau Point. We Phantom Ranch overnighters were sent off to do other things for a while, which mostly meant making a last-minute trip to the nearby pit toilet.

The sky was clearing within the Canyon as the first two groups started down; it could be a decent day after all. Our group consisted of four women and one man: two couples and a single, me. We quickly learned that the male, a retired educator from the Midwest, had lost 60 pounds over the last two years in order to do this mule trip! He brought up the rear of our line: his wife in front of him, the other two women came next, putting me right behind the wrangler.

Her name was Sherry, and she was a tiny, wiry young woman with a long braided blonde ponytail. We immediately trusted her implicitly; there was no choice! I tried not to fixate on the fact that my mule was named Short Cut, a tendency she has "mostly gotten over," Sherry assured me.

We started down the muddy trail, getting the feel for being up high on the back of a very large animal. Sherry stopped us at the top of the first switchback to check saddles and get our names down on a piece of paper. By then all the orientation instruction had come to life and we had questions about holding the reins and how to use the motivators, the whips that will urge the mules to keep moving in a tight grouping rather than lagging behind and then trying to catch up, which was so dangerous on a narrow trail with a sheer drop-off.

We continued along the three miles of trail I'd hiked; I was impatient to get to the levels I hadn't yet been close to: the Redwall, for instance, and down Jacob's Ladder, as the set of switchbacks through the Bright Angel Fault is called, to the wash that runs out to Indian Garden, our first prolonged stop.

With time out for a box-lunch break, we got off our mules with Sherry standing beside each of us in turn, to steady us. The first bit of relief was finding that my legs still worked…maybe I'd make it, after all.

When we were mounted up again, Sherry told us we were not quite even half way yet, and we began to worry again that we wouldn't be able to endure the plod through even the wash ahead. But at this elevation there were spring wildflowers to distract our attention, after too much winter up on the Rim. Stopped at a waterfall, I looked over my shoulder and asked about the trail dropping off a bluff…

"That's ours," Sherry confided. Oh. The others didn't see it until we began the grueling descent down the Devil's Corkscrew, a steep path through the Vishnu Schist.

Now the legs really felt it: it was as though I were trying to brake the mule like a car by bracing myself, with my legs taking the brunt of the downward part of the trip. By the time we finished crisscrossing Pipe Creek, where the water seemed to surprise the mules because otherwise it was dry so much of the time, the outside portion of my right knee had become excruciatingly painful, distracting me from the scenery. Bummer!

But the first sight of the Colorado River revived the awe, reminding us all of the point of the trip.

Sherry warned us not to get our hopes up at first sight of the suspension bridge over the river; it was not the one the mules used to cross. The black bridge with its covered flooring that mules will walk over was another two miles away.

The River trail to it went up and down as it wound along the rock formations of the Inner Canyon. Flowing below and beside us, the Colorado was in its original state: the red mud from the winter snowmelt gave the River its name.

I tried to focus on being grateful to have this rare treat, but mostly I was looking forward to getting through the tunnel (duck), across the black bridge, and on around the bend to Bright Angel Creek and finally to Phantom Ranch.

We made it! As Sherry helped each of us dismount, we staggered over to the rest area and bonded in our gratitude that we wouldn't have to get back on our mules for another two days...we were all two-nighters.

The ranch manager welcomed us. "The good news is you made it! The bad news is the water pipeline is broken so we're closing

Phantom Ranch tomorrow at 8 A.M. You'll have to go back up to the Rim tomorrow."

Our groans of disappointment nearly drowned out the advice to go out and hike so that our legs won't freeze up.

It was two in the afternoon; dinner would be at five: this left just three hours to see and do all that was planned for the full extra day down here. Where to start?

I headed for a trail that everyone said was a must for its views of the Ranch and River. Following the Bright Angel Creek northward, I cut off and started climbing up towards Clear Creek overlook. But while climbing higher and enjoying the high desert landscape, it suddenly hit me: all this time I'd been striving to get to the River. So why was I hiking up and away from it, for yet another distant view?!

Turning around and retracing my steps, I followed the creek back through Phantom Ranch, passing the hiker dorms, the canteen, the cabins, the shower house. There were a couple of tents in the campground. It was impressive that these handful of campers carried their equipment on their backs the whole way, some 18-plus miles round trip.

Craving solitude, I found an alcove of rock to crawl into. Breathe, just keep breathing, I reminded myself....quietly, so as to be able to hear the ancient silence of some of the oldest exposed rocks of our planet. But the trail was too popular; several other women came along and stopped to talk. I gave up and gave in, and followed them to the dining room.

Dinner consisted of huge slabs of steak, baked potatoes, salad and vegetables, corn bread and chocolate cake. Everything had been carried in on the backs of mules; all trash must likewise be carried back out. Sitting together on long tables in assigned groupings, we got to visit with others who had made this trip, either by foot or mule.

Stories were diverse and heroic, and most of the folks were over fifty, some were even sixty and others were well into their seventies: everyone who makes it here really had to make an effort, as the only ways in are by foot, by mule, or, in the warmer months, by raft. We were truly the chosen ones; those who have chosen to be here…taken the risks, endured the discomfort, and just plain been blessed.

Dinner was over early enough: there was still daylight, so I headed back to the River. Turning east towards the mule bridge, I wandered down onto the boat beach.

The sand was soft and cool and comforting on my bottom; the solitude and silence were delicious. Looking up the Canyon walls along the river corridor was like being in a womb/tomb enclosure….inhaling the scent of the nearby mud, I gave myself over to fully being here.

The sound of the water, the sight of the earth layers rising above me, the scent of the air, the aftertaste of dinner, the pervading sense of changing light all came together in a moment of deep meditation. And mystery. And magic!

Suddenly, great sobs welled up until I was shaking uncontrollably. A sense of being embedded within everything was so strong that I no longer knew where I ended and the sand and the River and the Canyon began. A supreme knowing of a wholeness akin to holiness swept through me with a relief that was stronger than the grief of all previous losses, disappointments, failures, frustrations.

As I let go to go into that place, a strange new power pervaded my being.

In the deep silence, I could hear the River pulsing through my own veins. I could feel the memory of the earth crouched deep within my own DNA. My own breaths interconnected me with the exhalations of the vegetation beside me.

And the light, the glorious, waning light from the sun became the same light from the very beginning of Time itself, reaching me just then. I was one with it all. All was a gift, wrapped up in a moment of grace.

This *grace-point* is the place where the mystics of all traditions live. As Huston Smith revealed in a lecture I attended in Berkeley: if you put the major religious traditions in side-by side-columns, then draw a line across them all about a third of the way down, this is the line where all the mystics sit, and from where they reflect upon the same Unitive experience.

How right they all were: Jung, Tillich, Emerson, the Hindu Sages. There *is* a Ground of Being, a central fire, an Oversoul, a Brahman. Their intuitive insights were as solid as Canyon walls!

Yet the reality of this Canyon was more actual than abstract, something as solid as a pebble I could hold in my hand, while simultaneously being held within the womb of the Universe.

As with all aha moments, this knowing started to fade as my mind began to wander, and my wonder turned into wondering.

Somewhere behind me, the Bright Angel Creek was tumbling down the Bright Angel Fault from the North Rim into the Colorado River; we had followed the Bright Angel Trail from the South Rim to reach this convergence that John Wesley Power named from a favorite Methodist hymn in his childhood.

*Shall we gather at the river,*
  *Where bright angel's feet have trod,*
*With its crystal tide forever,*
  *Flowing by the throne of God.*

Diane P. Freedman is the author of *Midlife with Thoreau: Poems, Essays, Journals,* a mixed-genre memoir (Hiraeth, 2015), and *An Alchemy of Genres: Cross-Genre Writing* by American Feminist Poet-Critics (Virginia). Her poems and essays have appeared several publications including: *Ascent, Permafrost, Roberson Poetry Annual, ISLE, Shorewirds, University of Dayton Review, Bucknell Review,* and *Crazyquilt.* She is editor or co-editor of *The Teacher's Body: Embodiment, Authority, and Identity in the Academy, Millay at 100: A Critical Reappraisal, The Intimate Critique: Autobiographical Literary Criticism,* and *Autobiographical Writing across the Disciplines: A Reader.* She is Professor of English and core faculty Member in Women's Studies at the University of New Hampshire.

# Wild Apple Associations

## by Diane P. Freedman

T HE OTHER DAY, my Modern Poetry professor showed some slides of still lives by Cezanne—mostly apples and oranges. They reminded me of my mother's painting, the one that hung in the dining room as long as I can remember. A light brown wood frame slightly askew surrounded a canvas mostly blue: a blue, draped cloth held a blue bottle daubed with white and bulging oranges and apples arranged on a distorted, falling-down, pale plate. It amazes me that I cannot recall the painting exactly; after all, I must have looked at it daily for fifteen years or more. I never did like the painting much, but I some-how deduced my mother had talent, or at least inclination, and it sometimes saddened me that she did not paint more or anymore.

Did she feel too much competition from my father? Back when my mother's painting was first displayed, Dad did not use oils. He sketched enthusiastically in charcoal or pencil, and he once took a class in marble sculpting. The distended head of a hefty marble woman still flanks our family fireplace. In the last four years or so, however, Dad has managed to cover over 300 canvases with oil paint. Twenty or thirty of these hang in the dining room, living room, kitchen, and bedrooms of the house in Long Island. The rest are stacked against one another in what was formerly a down-stairs laundry room or are displayed in our family vacation house in Vermont. Dad paints winter trees, Dickens' characters, *National Geographic* photographs, unflattering portraits of his wife and children, a few still-lives—no apples or oranges that I can recall—

and some lumpy landscapes that nonetheless move me when I am home visiting: I miss New England and New York, not quite feeling at home in the Pacific northwest where I live now.

Reading Thoreau's "Wild Apples" the same week that I viewed the Cezannes made me more homesick than ever—and suddenly my "home" became the whole of the east coast painted in my parents' pictures or depicted in the Emerson, Whitman, and Thoreau I have been reading for my classes in graduate school.

Thoreau spoke of longing to see a crabapple tree and of the beauty of wild apple blossoms and perfume. Reading him, I remembered the two crabapples in our backyard, Dad and me crabbing at one another, staging crabapple fights with my siblings and him. Misty, our pet Weimaraner, would leap into the arms of our eating-apple tree to pluck and eat the apples he loved so much. All the apple-family trees filled the air with pale pink blossoms in spring, while the plum and pear trees snowed the yard with white. I asked for a flowering cherry tree for my sixteenth birthday, and my mother used to mail me leaves and a Polaroid of that tree in blossom each spring I was away at college.

Farther from home than ever now, I find the large, watery, Red Delicious apples for which Washington state is famous disappointing. I search everywhere for an eastern McIntosh, a Cortland, a Rome Beauty. Living in upstate New York for college, for a total of eight years on and off, spoiled me; the only good apples here are the Gravensteins that grow in my new back yard, but they do not last. Unlike Thoreau, who did not mind insects in his wild apples, I mind the earwigs and the bees becoming drunk, hanging around too close to the house. To avoid bugs and the odor of sweet rot, I have to cart away hundreds of fallen bruised or half-eaten apples. I load up a plastic laundry basket and, under cover of darkness, discard my too-many apples in what passes for woods around here, some stranger's scruff near a driveway. The good apples we eat, or Moon, my new dog, eats, or I bake into pies. I feel bad about not using more of the apples, and the apples retaliate—thunking down on the roof or porch as we sleep, scaring even the dog awake.

It is funny to me that Thoreau so liked the smell of apples, new and old. I remember writing a poem about the scent of apples my sophomore year in college; then I thought rotting apples smelled like menstrual blood—I hated the smell, hated perhaps my own body and that of other women with whom, I am ashamed to say, I felt I had to compete for a man. I wrote:

## The Battle

Corpses of apples
in the backyard sun and brown grass;
central to these fruits
is their deadability
red and scented like menstrual blood
(sickeningly sweet somewhere
along the line).

I am not the first doll;
I am among
the girls holding the doll case
on which there is a girl holding
a doll case on...my Betsy-McCall doll case.
I am off in some little-windowed
room, taking only very small steps

towards opening the glass pane/pain.

Apple-cheeked doll-girl that I am,
choosing warm red lips,
being choked now, Sleeping Beauty,
by indecision on everyone's part:

all of me wants to play beyond
the closed yard of three feet
by three feet, the triangle.
Being shown an apple a day will not keep me away;
before too much sun dries my seeds brown,
she will be shaken from her rest...

I am red and green knowing how
to stem myself
into versus...

What does this line of thought I am tracing from Cezanne's out-of-proportion paintings, to my mother's somewhat ungainly art, my father's big-headed woman and stretched-out versions of his children in oils, to Thoreau's perhaps exaggerated fondnesses, to my collegiate jealousies, and my contemporary memories say about the knowledge apples impart or the associations they may generate? I do not how much space (proportionately) or what kind of fanfare to give this—and pardon my punning: I see that proportion and perspective are as difficult and as full of relatives as any family tree.

William Henry Searle, born 1987, awarded a PhD in Creative Writing and Environmental Philosophy. Author of *Lungs of my Earth: A Personal Ecology*, published by Hiraeth Press. Work has appeared in *Resurgence, Bellevue Literary Review, Earthlines*, and elsewhere, and endorsed by thinkers and writers such Satish Kumar, Joanna Macy, Sir Andrew Motion, and others. His piece, "Living in the Shadow of the Rain," was finalist in the Barry Lopez Creative Nonfiction Award. His is currently working on his next book, *Landscapes of Kin*.

# 3,000 Metres

## *A Walk at Height with My Father*

### by William Henry Searle

Place always opens a region in which it gathers the things
in their belonging together...
–Martin Heidegger

He is my father, my father,
And from him all I gather
Are things that he allows...
–Andrew Motion

*Becs des Bossons* Sunrise

D AD, IN HIS OLIVE-GREEN AND INDIGO CHEQUERED
NIGHT-SHIRT, leans out of the top window of the
Cabane des Becs-de-Bossons; a two-storey mountain
hut perched at a lone position upon the edge of a wide and undulate
col, 2,980 metres above sea level, in the Pennine Alps of southern
Switzerland. I am standing outside, wrapped in my down jacket.
We are both looking eastward. We are waiting for sunrise.

There is a rising sharpness to the dark that, as it dispels, carves
out near and far things into gradually stunning relief. Flowers,
ones with names I know and ones of which I am ignorant, sparsely
surround my boots in ground-hugging dispersion. I bend and rub
the intangible petal of a flower between finger and thumb, its form
barely visible in the half-dark, and is contained in a sleep of indolent

purple. The flowers dream of their fulfilment in the forthcoming sun. There is no wind as such, only cool eddies of air that roll and spiral in small acrobatics, then become still, and vanish. Scattered embryonic wind. My senses fumble for themselves. Dad has never been so hushed. The land places a finger across its lips. We listen. As I look up to my immediate left at Dad who has not moved, his forearms crossed beneath his chest that is opened out a fraction, his head up, leaning forward, he points commandingly to the east. The first light. A narrow funnel of pale crimson floats down through two adjacent snowy mountains, and fills the dark valley beyond with a light that is both gentle and awesome, then lifts, lifts, broadening and warming to diaphanous gold tinged with whites and vermillion. We become more motionless. I want to thank Dad for not allowing me to miss this first light. He has closed his eyes as though to concentrate more fully on breathing in the splendor. And the sky blooms into a euphoria of frosted blues. The sun feels itself out into the earth. My senses find themselves. Today is our final mountain.

I

Pfulroe, 3,300 metres

Our first mountain. At 3,000 metres the mist shifts, revealing a circle of blue sky ahead through which pokes the tops of mountains. Up to our left beneath a dark cliff, chamois forage around the base of immaculate erratics. We watch the animals for a while, though they are far away. Their hooves clatter and tinkle through scree. From our distance they look like Chinese Water Deer.

Spider-threads are moored from one rock to the other in glistening gossamer patterns which, reflecting the sunlight above and the snow beneath, seem unreal and evoke pauses of puzzlement in us all. Even the guide is stopped in his tracks by the delicate networks of spider webs, an acre of reticulated iridescence, sloping down over the boulders to the darker regions below the snow line. We stare, gawk even. Dad is cautious not to break them but in doing so he jeopardies his balance, and slips. I do not want to break the silken craft-work either, but it is unavoidable. They tear across our shins as we regretfully mow through them.

Dad and I lunge up together onto the summit, and step down onto ice stiffened snow. I have to close my eyes in the blinding radiance of the sky and snow. For a moment, I turn dizzy with exasperation, then open my eyes in a state of disbelief at the awesomeness of the surrounding vista. My body is blown open beyond coherence. My breathing is out of step with my heart-beat that thumps out of sync with my eyes that wince before the silence which my ears cannot flee from. I look away from the delighted expressions of the group towards my own point on the horizon, a lapis cliff hung with snow. In that I am gathered. Dad and I sip water from our flasks, and eat chocolate.

## II
### Hornli Hut, 3,260 metres

THE HEMP-BROWN ROPE-RAIL, scuffed and whiskered by countless trafficking of hands, yanks taught under the weight of our ascending group. A yard in front of me the night-club bouncer from Leeds, brought here by a restless yearning to revel in wild travail, stomps with a gait of wired adolescence. His jacket sides brush against protruding swords of gneiss and ophiolite rock. His breathing, though, is measured. Five yards behind me and increasing, Dad is alternating between uneven strides to close the distance between us and an almost static walk. He is cursing. He yells that it helps to fire him up. He seems angry at the mountain, the Matterhorn.

Clag boils up from behind aretes in strobe acts of terrific surprise, sails in over us like the ghosts of grey pack ice meeting in another life, and pursues itself in lattice-wending purls and reams of unfurling fog chasing itself through the air with unnerving speed. The Matterhorn knows we are here.

I look back and Dad isn't moving at all. The mountain is slipping away beneath him like a sand dune surfaced in black volcanic sand. Too soon he is out of sight. The rope-rail is tugging back tight, creaking, in his grab, sagging under release to low U dips that make me worry that he's lost. Then the rope tightens. The clag, restricting vision to no more than a metre, is claustrophobic and eerie.

Watching him emerge, finally, from the coiling rolls of fog, still cursing and panting, into this confined and massive space where I wait, is mysteriously poignant. His familiarity is settling. Here we find each other beyond the categories of father and son, at the juncture where two real lives converge.

Together we ascend the last cut-back of the trail, into snow-fall, as dusk and mist and snow concoct to make a fluid darkness like that of the sea at night. A single lit window through the darkness holds us momentarily in awe. The hut. Our tryst has brought on shared leases of life, like tributaries churning into one course, gathered into a current that is far more than both of them combined, and older, as old as the mountain upon whose shoulder we are bourne.

## III
### Bella Tolla, 3,025 metres

BLOOD-PINK STAINS OF SAHARAN DUST are speckled throughout patches of east-facing snow. An alpine lake glistens, awash with flies as light as castings of grass seed. Dad is chatting with the guide. There is a lightness to the mood of the group this morning that is a rebellion against the heavy darkness of yesterday, blissful even. A sense of camaraderie, of companionship, has naturally developed over the week, without intrusions and the pressure to know the ins and outs of each other's personal lives. We know enough of each other to know that we can share in the walk, to expect no offense, to be ease with one another. We find each other. A moving community founded on a pattern of respect and love for where we are. Our desires concord here. I succumb to a filial happiness that is as concrete as the rocks, the sky, and the lake that transfixes our gaze in the target of its azure eye.

Thirty meters of harsh ascent shy of the summit, we stop and glug water. It is hot. Dad and I remove extraneous layers, as do the others, the guide. The massif of mountains to the south is an altar, the sense of which has been earned. I do not have any other words for today except that life, here, the pinnacled beginning of it, has come full circle. I am as close to Dad as I ever will be and have been. The preciousness of this intimacy brims to the sky.

## IV
### Becs des Bosson Ascent 3,149 meters

LEAVING BEHIND SUNRISE, we make our way up our final 3,000m summit of the week. Choss-scree like beach shingle and shattered slabs of honeycomb, crunch under my heel, rattles free, skitters down over the ledge of a precipitous ravine, the sounds of the shingle shower swallowed by the falls of silence. Looping around stands of sedimentary rocks too brittle to gain confident purchase, the hands crimping hesitantly, ducking under arches, squeezing sideways through clefts dark and cool—the mountain is an almost vertical maze. There are obstacles at every turn. The palms of my hands are dusted with the grain of the stone. It is like wandering through an elaborately structured home, drawn in further in search of the home's hearth, its centre, down corridors, through rooms and hallways, designed to lose you to itself. The architecture of the mountain is deeply playful. I cannot get enough of it.

At the foot of a ten-foot wall of bright schist, we hoist one another up by the rungs of foot and thigh, onto the summit which is too narrow to accommodate more than one person at a time. Dad goes first. His strong hands seek rock holds as I and another push him upwards from underneath his boots, our hands cradled around his soles. He kicks and scuffles up, and propels himself onto the summit. And steps off out of sight, into the blue sky. I hope up there he takes all the time he really needs to let where he is and what he is sink into him and lift him out. Our waiting for his call to help him down is like the waiting after prayer.

*Barrage de Moiry*

O N A FATIGUED HIGH, the week's trek over, the group returned to their workaday lives, Dad and I stay on for one more day, catch the bus from Grimentz to see the Barrage de Moiry.

Upon a café terrace built into the top wall of the dam, we gaze out across the reservoir, towards the mountains. The day is turned to its highest intensity of colours. Flowers, the snow, the blue of the lake, exhale. Whilst drinking ice tea, Dad hands me a sprig of edelweiss, ivory green coated with a translucent fur, which he nabbed from a flower-pot upon the café's exterior windowsill. It is rare and beautiful, symbolic of so much I cannot fathom. A gift I marvel at. We break bread amidst bright flowers.

The day after tomorrow the demands of the daily nine-to-five will sap his energies, close him up. And we will see each other now and again with a partition of aloofness unknowingly put up between us, and these mountains, this place, a partition that neither of us can bring down without the strength of the land. But there won't be time nor space enough for such intervention. We will be robbed of an understanding of our ourselves, of each other, that this week has garnered. The strict round of how things convention achieves itself upon will reclaim us. If we are not careful this week will dwindle into an inconsequential hallucination of what is possible. We will flounder, prisoners of marginal existence, in scripted hours maintained by society's curriculum of profane toil.

Dad, let not this walk pale away into a mere holiday, an unreal foray. Let us not forget what holds us. Once home, I will put the sprig of edelweiss in a safe place. And the image of you placing the flower in my open hand I will press between the central pages of my heart.

Francesca G. Varela is the author of two young-adult novels, *Call of the Sun Child*—a bronze medalist in the 2014 Moonbeam Children's Book Awards—and *Listen*. Francesca recently graduated from the University of Oregon with degrees in Environmental Studies and Creative Writing. When not writing, she spends her time practicing piano and violin, figure skating, walking her dog, Ginger, and exploring Oregon's wild places.

www.francescavarela.com

# If the Stars Should Appear
## by Francesca G. Varela

AS MY SHOES CRUNCHED AGAINST THE GRAVELLY SOIL, brushed porcelain in the moonlight, I couldn't help but think of who else might be awake. Mountain lions, coyotes, black bears, bobcats. The rest of the group was far behind me now, our circle of tents hidden among the salal bushes and the tufts of yarrow. The great ponderosa pines were blue, all their needles wippling in the wind like a field of grass. *Shh*, they said, *shh*, so I thanked them for their guidance.

I liked to think that if I met a bobcat or a bear, we might stare at each other for a long, quiet moment, then stalk away, each in our own direction, both of us overly conscious of the other's footsteps. But as I walked alone I thought of all the stories I'd heard; the girl, parked on the side of the highway, who was bitten in the leg by a cougar when she stepped out of the car; the woman who was mauled by a pack of coyotes on a city running trail; the boy who was attacked by a bear in his own backyard.

It was a cold night, cold and dry and clear. I clenched my hands together. With this full moon I could see everything, albeit faded, soft, versions, like the forest had dulled out beneath the sea. I had to admit, I was a little angry with the moon. We were far enough away from the city that I'd been expecting stars. Millions upon millions, all overrun with the cinnamon warmth of the Milky Way. That was the thing; I'd never seen the Milky Way, and now my chance was blasted over with the light of a full moon. The same thing had happened before. Backpacking along the coast, it was too cloudy. The central cascades were more diluted than I'd expected, with enough light pollution to weaken the sky. It seemed that the stars, the real, enormous, cacophonous spread of deep space and galaxy dust, would be forever hidden from me.

Of course I'd seen pictures of the Milky Way, but sometimes I wondered if it even really looked like that. I'd heard stories of friends going night-kayaking in Puget Sound, seeing the stars leap into the dark and solid water, and I'd heard about lying on wool blankets in the high desert, the shrubland receding like something hidden, cool and tight inside a basement chest. How they watched the sky for hours, unable to pick out the constellations from all the small stars they'd forgotten about but had always missed. I doubted that the real Milky Way would live up to those chiseled, ink-lined images my imagination had formed, wherein the sky seemed to quiver with all the movement of breathing stars.

And I wouldn't be finding out on this trip. That was my punishment for forgetting to count the moon phases.

I rotated my gaze between my hiking boots and that boisterous moon, glancing occasionally behind me—just in case. Every so often I heard water, or maybe wind; a quiet, feathery sound that sadly reminded me of a highway of cars.

There was a field just ahead, a clearing rough with twigs and small brush. Earlier that day I'd walked there, through filigreed, blooming snowbrush; the yellow flowers of arrowleaf balsam root; the lengthy tracts of bracken ferns. All along the field there had been little treelings. Some of them barely reached above the plump stalks of grass, whose seeds were fluffed out and waiting for me to knock them.

In the moonlight the field looked much smaller. The encumbered ground crunched bluntly beneath me. All this noise seemed sacrilegious in the presence of the night sky. I wanted to remain only a whisper, to hear little else but the trees scraping against the wind, and perhaps the click of an owl or some other night bird watching over the field.

I'd been hoping to see at least a few stars there, maybe near the horizon, their light sharpened through tree branches. Right away I picked out Vega, and a heavy dot that was either Jupiter or Venus. Otherwise the sky was empty. It was the palest shade of black, almost blue. For a moment I focused only on that emptiness. I thought back to the day my family had driven to a forested lake, stayed there all day, past sunset, just to show me the stars. The moon had outshone them then, too. As we drove home I asked to pull over. Just a little longer. Maybe it wasn't dark enough yet. Maybe the stars would soon surface. I stood on a patch of grass along the side of the road, next to a blinking small-town construction sign. The air was still hot, rising from the pavement. I didn't know when I'd have another chance. We didn't leave the city lights often. All there was was the moon. The orange moon of early fall, and, tonight, the clear moon of early summer.

All along its rim the moon was almost pink. This moon was not cold, but a white fire, or perhaps the melted reflection of a mountain. I always wondered what ancient people thought the moon was. Something powerful, something punctual, something covered in dark gray seas. Whatever they thought of it, the moon had always held meaning for nearly all people. And it still did. I found it hard to believe that anyone could not be moved by the ghosted moonlight on their arms.

Suddenly the bushes creaked. Silence—and then it came again. I remembered the cougars, bobcats. In a quick-footed flurry I dashed over the baby trees and returned to my path in the forest. The safety of tents and people was so far off. I felt like something was behind me. Still jogging, I looked back, and there was the moon again, steady, calm.

In that moment I asked the moon for protection. The sky, the sun, the sea, the earth; all things great and mysterious, anything that floated with the cycles of life, seemed capable of lending its own strength through the shared components of our being, the ancient kinship of energy. And right there, right then, I had the moon with me.

In that moment of panic, of helplessness, I thought I understood why the first religions had formed. A sense of control over the uncontrollable, yes, but perhaps there was more to it than that. Perhaps the moon really was protecting me, just by comforting me, and by guiding me safely to my tent. And for the first time I was glad that I had the moon with me instead of the Milky Way. The stars would have been lost as I ran. They would have been tangled in the trees. In all their glorious, distant mystery, they would have left me. But the moon—the moon would follow me anywhere. And, perhaps, I thought, I would follow it as well.

David K. Leff is an essayist and poet and former deputy commissioner of the Connecticut Department of Environmental Protection. He is the author of four nonfiction books, three collections of poetry, and a novel in verse. *Maple Sugaring: Keeping it Real in New England* is his latest book (Wesleyan, 2015). *Canoeing Maine's Legendary Allagash: Thoreau, Love, and Survival of the Wild*, a memoir about a backcountry river trip is due out from Homebound in 2016.

www.davidkleff.com

# Birdwatching
## *Not Just for the Birds*
### by David K. Leff

Oh, the Places You'll Go
–Dr. Seuss

PERHAPS THERE'S SOMETHING PECULIAR about wandering through a cemetery in dim predawn light while paying just brief attention to gravestones. Of course, it's no stranger than spending time at the historical society without interest in the past, or visiting community gardens in late December among dead and desiccated plantings long after harvest. But such excursions are typical for birdwatchers. There's a lot more to birdwatching than watching birds.

Though I'm somewhat middling at bird identification, I recognize a fair number of species and thrill to the uncertainty searching. In an age of increasingly planned lives, you never know what you'll find when looking for birds. But at least as much as birdwatching, I enjoy the company of birdwatchers. They live in a state of constant anticipation that is both contagious and inspiriting.

Birdwatchers are non-contact hunters of sorts, prowling about, senses on high alert for their quarry. It's no surprise that the oldest, most celebrated birdwatching event, the Audubon Christmas bird count, began in 1900 as a hunting alternative. Stealth, consciousness, and perceptual acuity is more important than a good pair of binoculars. Birders are sensitive to color, movement, weather, shape, and sound. They look at the relationship of birds to the places they visit, knowing that certain trees, fruits and seeds, topographical features, or human presences such as dumpsters or ditches are likely places for particular species. They venture out at hours most people don't regularly experience—at first light for spring songsters or deep into a chilly night for owls. Intrepid by nature, birders are intimate with rain, fog, searing heat, and frigid, snowy days.

Sure, it's a bit strange to be traipsing through Hartford's Cedar Hill Cemetery in the early morning gloaming giving only a passing nod to the dead. But that's what it takes to see a great horned owl explode from a thicket of spruce while you watch in startled awe as seven deer calmly graze nearby. No disrespect to J.P. Morgan, Katherine Hepburn, Wallace Stevens and other notables buried here, but it's more the vibrancy of birdsong than their eternal quiet that draws my interest, at least for today.

Among the few wild creatures persisting in the face of human development, birds take me to unexpected places for unusual reasons at odd times. As is customary, the December 2015 Hartford Christmas count began among Cedar Hill's gravestones under a brightening sky with quickly moving cumulous clouds. Atypically warm, temperatures were in the 40s. Along with a clutch of fellow enthusiasts, I next stopped at nearby Goodwin Park golf course. At the only time I am likely to spend on the links there are no golfers, but with ponds and close cropped lawns the course is perfect habitat for Canada geese. Hundreds were on the water, along with a few mallards, and even more congregated on the gently rolling fairways dotted with grand trees that seemed sculptural without their leaves. There were also lots of gulls.

In the heart of downtown, we stood on Main Street, binoculars focused on the 527 foot-tall Travelers office tower in the hope of sighting peregrine falcons. Although they had appeared in previous years, on this day we saw only the tower's intricate architectural details, invisible to the naked eye. Sadly, the female was killed not long ago, crashing into a wall while chasing pigeons. It appears that the roost is now empty. Instead of peregrines, we counted house sparrows on the sidewalk and pigeons perched without fear on nearby buildings.

The Connecticut River at Riverside Park was broad and slow. Surprisingly we saw no waterfowl and the tangled floodplain woods punctuated with large silver maples yielded only a few sparrow-like "chipping" sounds, so we made haste to the now closed Hartford landfill sandwiched between I-91 and the river.

Escorted by an official of the agency that operated the landfill for many years, we rambled around the plateau-like top rising 130 feet above its surroundings, offering dramatic views of Hartford and the Connecticut valley. We made our way into declivities at the edge, and along the dike paralleling the river. Our big find was a lone Savannah sparrow, a fairly uncommon lover of grasslands. Soon afterward, we sighted about 40 horned larks, brown birds larger than sparrows with black and yellow facial features. They also favor open fields.

Hartford's landfill epitomized the day's experience—that nature is not separate from human involvement. Over time, "natural" has largely become a joint enterprise between civilization and wildness. Only a few years ago, gulls scavenging the garbage were by far the most numerous species. Raptors feeding on rodents that inhabited the mound were more common. Now that the landfill is closed and seeded to become a field, it's a significant home for grassland birds. Gulls are virtually nonexistent, and although we spotted a couple red-tailed hawks, a kestrel, and a Cooper's hawk, birds of prey are less common than they once were. More than our debasement of the environment, the landfill illustrates our close, inseparable connection to nature.

For something wholly different, we drove down densely urban Main Street in Hartford's north end to count house sparrows, starlings, and pigeons, ninety-six of which perched on the venerable Weaver Building. Before long we were walking among the warren of fenced community gardens behind the tent-like modernist architecture of the Unitarian Church at the city's western edge. The last harvest had been many weeks ago and all the cultivators were long gone. We were looking for birds gleaning the remains of fruits, seeds and vegetables the gardeners had left behind among the dried out, khaki stems that once yielded produce. There were many birds foraging among the leftovers, including blue jays, tree and song sparrows, juncos, gold and house finches.

Eschewing a fabulous archive and exhibits about the past, we next wandered the wooded margins of the Connecticut Historical Society grounds along the brushy, twisting banks of the Park River where we saw birds common at winter feeders—titmice, juncos and house sparrows. Just few blocks away, our next stop at Elizabeth Park with its well kept lawns and gardens beneath tall shade trees yielded an entirely different experience. After counting mallards in the park pond, we were drawn to a repeated high pitched *queeah, queeah, queeah* sounding from a large oak. We trained our binoculars on a red-headed woodpecker, its crimson head glowing electrically in the late afternoon light. Increasingly uncommon, it was the find of the day and we stood transfixed, staring at it for about fifteen minutes as if to make sure we had actually seen it and forgetting any other birding in the park. The sun was starting to set and we made quickly for our last and probably most unlikely stop.

Our birding odyssey concluded in the vast asphalt parking lot of a supermarket on a street busy with fast food restaurants, gas stations and other such enterprises. We'd come to count crows flying to nighttime roosts. At first we'd spot two or three, maybe a dozen winging in the gathering dusk. But as it grew darker, much larger flocks appeared, almost more birds than three people could count. Soon there was a river of the coal black corvids above us as shoppers navigated carts among cars and drove away unaware of the exhilarating phenomena in the dark sky. Crows may not be much to look at, but several thousand flying overhead in about twenty minutes is unforgettable.

We made our way home in a state of exhausted joy at seeing forty-something species in places few people associate with nature. There was disappointment in not spotting a peregrine, curiosity at the paucity of starlings, excitement at spending so much time in the presence of a red-headed woodpecker. I marveled at the depth of wild mystery and wonder manifest in urban spaces near at hand.

But in this preternaturally warm season, our adventure was also a cautionary tale. Driving by the state armory just before dawn, we'd heard a robin belting out its spring mating song, and later spotted another yanking a worm from a lawn. Regardless of the politics and science of climate change, there is something unsettling, if not frightening about such out of cycle observations. It's just another reason to continue returning to these places year after year, keeping up with what birds are telling us about changes in our world.

Over the course of his life, James Scott Smith has lived in Michigan, Massachusetts, Kansas, California and for the last 23 years, Colorado. He studied psychology and religion while beginning his work with children and families as a psychotherapist, a wilderness guide, and a spiritual leader. He went on to create and lead a system of learning organizations designed to deliver holistic, experiential intervention in traditional and alternative settings. Breaking from his formal career in 2006, James enjoys his family and home life, the Colorado backcountry, his dogs, photography and writing. His first collection of poems, *Water, Rocks and Trees* is scheduled for release in September, 2016.

www.dogwalkerjames.wordpress.com

# Voyageur

## A Poetic Offering by James Scott Smith

I HAVE LIVED ENOUGH TO NO LONGER TELL A RIVER FROM A POEM. This is most fitting for a fly fisherman with an instinct for words. For more than a half-century the echoes of my childhood spent wandering along lakeshores in the North Woods of Ontario, Canada still ring in the water, rocks and trees of Colorado's legendary South Platte. A day spent striving to align my senses with fish is a kind of primal homecoming, a way of being ageless, naïve, wide-eyed. The only thing like it is being there when a poem rises and suddenly I am struggling to ease it out of the depths, to see it into its own and then, let it go.

## Of Poems and Rivers

I am
of poems and rivers.
I stand
as it all
works around
my footing.
I am held,
wordless
and watchful.
While I fish,
while I write,

waiting on delight,
a fight,
not knowing
what's next,
a broad turn
downstream,
a desperate run
to hidden structures,
a sudden gasp at
twisting flight then
plunging to
dark freedom.
I am
of poems and rivers,
immersed,
worked upon,
smoothed, and
someday
carried off,
to be found.

AVING DONE ALL WE COULD TO KEEP OUR CHILDREN close to each their own souls, to the earth, to water, to real places, including home, we now have reached this salient moment. There is no better symbol for passage into higher, wider realms than ancient waters. This is where we go to be born, to venture forth, to give birth, to raise the progeny, to prosper, and someday, to die. When children leave home they will be christened in a waterside ceremony of departure, as we remain rooted in the ways we should. All the while, the wildness informs the spirit of the wayfarer young and old alike, and like no other companion or comforter could.

## Bound Away

Their rivers have surged too
strong for this familiar dale, their
currents coursing to broader
valleys and further seas.
Being is an empty absolute, for now is
to do,
to task,
to venture outwardly on the
who
they will become. We send them
wrapped in prayers with songlines
from our brighter dreams. We
fly our flags unfurled and
keep our fears to burn in our own
fires. Though breaking hard

on grief we wait as they ascend the
mountain alone to drink from
ancient headwaters and quest along the
sacred, dangerous places.
God is asking much of us, so
we summon our faith with
hope they learn to live 'longside the
wolf we call this beautiful world.
Only then will they draw their
sustenance from the vernal spring that
flows of both the minerals and the
spirits, the earth and the sky.
That is what this work of love is for.

S TANDING IN THE WATER, I engage a complex ecosystem while asking the primordial spirits just one little question; what are they taking? I am one part scientist and two parts shaman. I watch big Browns nibble at microscopic bugs scuttling from beneath my boots. I marvel at clouds of sunlit, swirling hatches rising and falling, living and dying in a matter of minutes. I begin slowly to learn the ways of insects, their life cycle, and nuanced physical characteristics. Then, the deeper lore, born in dark places and storied at the level of the heart comes to shape my consciousness well outside the range of surface considerations.

## Emerger

Beneath the stone,
encased in stillness, dark and cool,
larvae strains to pupae strains
to nymph, then bubbled for transport
rising, emerging, surfacing,
enticing Browns and Rainbows suspended.
Resting, waiting, upon the flow then
spreading anxious into first
flutter, an embodied gasping for
first exchange, struggling
into the thinner, dryer, warmer medium,
fluttering, lifting,
falling, fluttering, lifting
falling, fluttering, lifting… flying
in spinning allurement of those below, and now
still rising

against the yellow sky,
belonging to it and everything,
the wind now leading
to the green love of willow brush
and resting again,
set above,
alongside
the depths once known.

W ILDNESS IS NOT ABOUT WHERE I LIVE, but rather, what is living within me. There have been times when faith was all there was to burn in the fire. There have been times when life's outward disappointments sang like sirens, calling me to paddle toward the shore of convention or compromise. Circumstances and wandering have taken me far and yon over decades since my early ordination in the unity. Yet even in the hardness of urbanity, or the dryness of trite or quaint cultural immersion, wildness always comes looking for it's own, rising from within, carrying out and away, homeward to the primal domain, the good world from which I come and to which I will return.

## Voyageur

He is of the North, and
prays in the way of
water and fire, elements of
journey, paddling through
an expanse of vanquish,
ravaged by love unrequited,
on voyage many years,
passage and portage, the
depths on one side,
the forest on the other,
a darkening mystery
below and above. Each
offer their bounty to the
North man for body and spirit

to subsume in creaturely endurance
and in the broader narrative; bestowments
of the wild God. He lies alone, fireside,
out under the stars
and near to his thoughts
on the suffering of the world,
his loneliness, and the
common yearning found in all
creation for some sense of
consummation that is always yet ahead,
not fully known, the great hunger
shared by all in striving forward
for survival or significance. No one
rests but for the dead.
He dreams of returning
home, taking his woman into his
arms, drawing her alongside his
desires by the small of her strong
back, waiting for her to sense
her yes to him, her wanting him
as much. For now, he might
be more starbound than within her, for
he has been lost to himself for so long.
In the dawn, he eats his fish and
wild mushrooms, blueberries
on his oats, chased down by black coffee.
He reads his Jeffers as clear as a man
ever could and aches for the
despair of it. In setting off

with the new day,
in faith that knows
nothing, he has the water and
the fire, and for now
he can only be sure
he is being led.

Eric D. Lehman teaches literature and creative writing at the University of Bridgeport and his essays, reviews, poems, and stories have been published in dozens of journals and magazines. He is the author of eight history books, including *Homegrown Terror: Benedict Arnold and the Burning of New London*, and *Becoming Tom Thumb: Charles Stratton, P.T. Barnum, and the Dawn of American Celebrity*, which won the Henry Russell Hitchcock Award from the Victorian Society of America and was chosen as one of the American Library Association's outstanding university press books of the year. He is also the author of the bestselling travel guide *Insiders' Guide to Connecticut*, the Pushcart-nominated memoir *Afoot in Connecticut: Journeys in Natural History*, and the short story collection, *The Foundation of Summer*.

# The Way the Earth Feels About Your Feet

by Eric D. Lehman

ONE WINTER DURING THE LONELY SINGLE YEARS of my late twenties, I began to track animals. After a snowfall it is remarkably easy: following a squirrel to its nest or a herd of deer to its bed is just a matter of persistence, of slow and steady off-trail hiking, watching for the next depression in the white powder. At first it was just a nice way to explore, to have purpose when wandering the woods, much the way golf is a nice excuse for a walk on manicured grass.

But I liked it enough to get a few books on the subject: Ellsworth *Jaeger's Tracks and Trailcraft*, Len McDougall's *Complete Tracker*, Tom Brown's *Science and Art of Tracking*, and a variety of field guides. I quickly found that tracking without snow was a much bigger challenge. However, without straining myself in study and practice I learned the different animal tracks. I could soon distinguish the prints of a coyote from a dog, and could distinguish rubs and scratches from "natural occurrences" —really just other kinds of tracks.

On one fine winter Sunday, I walked out the door of my basement apartment and into the bare winter woods adjoining the Farmington Canal Trail. It was a small patch, only a few acres, in between some houses and a small warehouse, created by Shepard's Brook tumbling down over the stones of an old mill dam. A long swampy channel created a home for ducks, and a few old heaps of dirt from the canal's creation in the 1820s pretended to be real hills. On the banks of the backwater I found a set of tracks imprinted on the hard mud. At first I thought the small long-fingered front and larger hind paws might be muskrat, but then I noted that the forepaws had five toes and ended in claw marks. Probably a raccoon. I followed the trail along the bank, across a short section of leaf litter where I only spotted one track, and onto the bank of the rippling stream, where the strangely human-like hand prints led into the water. I looked directly across the stream into an elliptical hole in the steep hill-like bank, just below the backyards of a few houses. Waiting patiently on a small rock, I ate a can of sardines, and the smell did what I hoped. A little masked face poked right out of the hole and looked at me.

Encounters like this increased my dedication. I created quizzes for myself while reading, and took them several days later to be sure I retained the lore. I practiced plaster-casting a track to identify and preserve it. I occasionally made and studied human tracks in a sandbox and on the beach. I started thinking about some of my other activities as tracking—after all what is identifying a two-hundred-year-old stone wall other than reading the track of a long-ago farmer?

Then I signed up for a weeklong course run by Tom Brown, Jr. His books were both the most spiritual and the most scientific, teaching the secrets of pressure releases—a technical method of categorizing, identifying, and following tracks. He also wrote a number of narrative books filled with what some might describe as outlandish stories of his exploits surviving in the wilderness and tracking fugitives. I enjoyed those even more, but I wanted to go beyond reading about someone else's adventures. I wanted to make my own more possible.

So, one Sunday in June I drove down to the New Jersey Pine

Barrens, and after parking at a shopping center was taken by van through twisty sand roads through the scrub, pines to the large survival camp. I set up my tent, brushed ticks off my legs, and found a seat in the large open lecture hall underneath a nest of wrens. The dozens of other attendees included wildlife biologists, martial artists, zombie apocalypse survivalists, park rangers, and Marines. They all had different reasons for being there—some wanted to learn how to build survival shelters or identify wild edibles, others want to learn how to tan animal hides or produce stone tools. Various experts gave lectures and we practiced various skills: carving a bow-drill set, building a solar still, making cordage out of Raffa using a reverse wrap technique. "A backpacker is like a scuba diver," Brown told us. "Learning to survive is taking off the scuba gear and breathing underwater."

Finally, on Tuesday morning he taught us the first lesson on tracking. At one point he stood on a table and showed us how breathing and other small movements changed the pressure on the feet, changed the tracks. It was a startling performance. But more importantly, he began to get across the importance of tracking, what it could mean for your life. It's not just a way to find animals, it is a way to see nature, to see the world. It heightens awareness, the way spiritual practice or scientific observation do. In fact, it remains somewhere between those two disciplines, part art, part science, and more elusive than either. He had said as much in his books, of course, but for the first time it clicked.

As towhees and red squirrels played in the camp around us and hummingbirds zipped through the open hall, we learned dozens of primary pressure releases, and dozens of secondaries. Digital and lobular pressure releases followed, and soon it became clear that the combinations were practically infinite, only made more manageable by this system of terms and measurements. "Pressure releases are the way the earth feels about your feet," Brown told us. We discussed ridges, peaks, waves, disks, dishes, crumbles, fissures, explode-offs, and combinations thereof, all of which he showed us in a large tracking pit of sand, to make it easier to see what he was talking about. Having someone teach me, show me, how a man with a full belly doing a head roll to the left made a different track than one with an empty belly looking right was obviously different than reading about it, and I learned more in a few hours there than I had in months of private study. Brown claimed he could see by a track if someone was sick, and after this demonstration I believed it.

On Thursday morning he set up a "tracking line" before breakfast, casually marking out a long line of different animal tracks along the old 1761 cannon road that led past the lecture hall. He began the process by showing a track to the first person, then moving on to the next track with the next person. Then the first person to see each track would show everyone else who came down the line. All the tracks he picked had been made in the previous eighteen hours, to demonstrate what has gone on underneath our noses in camp. "If it's not flat, it's a track," he tells us. "Debris doesn't create sequences and series." Many of the tracks were not in soil, but on moss or pine needles or leaves, each marked with a small popsicle stick designating the animal and which foot it was. We examined the prints of fox, rabbits, raccoons, shrews, squirrels, cats, and more—maybe seventy-five small, imperfectly perfect tracks that he had picked out in less than an hour. And these were just the ones along one side of the sandy road, not further into the bush, where a "world of tracks" awaited.

It was one of the most amazing things I had ever seen, and those stories Brown told in his books were suddenly not so outlandish. He could see tracks everywhere, as quickly as we could see live animals. This was beyond skill; this was close to being a superpower. Two days later he taught us the secret of dust and grit compressions, of making sure the light was at the right angle and letting the contrast between the shiny and the dull surfaces show us the track. We each pressed a pinky lightly on a leaf, and then held it up to the correct angle of light, seeing the print. Later, in a rare quiet moment by myself, I watched a spider walk across the Pine Barrens sand, and over what to him must have been a cliff. Then, getting my head close to the ground without disturbing the grains of sand, I found those tiny, tiny tracks, including three deeper ones where the arachnoid legs held on to the edge of the miniature bluff.

I wish I could say that I gained a superpower and that I am now able to read the tracks of ants across bare rock, identify the guests from last night's party by their muddy bootprints on the porch, or spot the month-earlier hoppings of a rabbit in the leaf litter. But in the years following I had a full-time job to think about, along with a writing career and a dozen other interests to keep me busy. To become a master at any art takes years and years of constant, dedicated practice, and tracking was not the one I chose to pursue. Yet even though my skills degrade with every hour I fail to spend in the bush, I never lose interest in following a trail. Even though I've never reached the level of master tracker, I can show my wife two deer prints in the leaf debris and explain how the animals took a drink from an old gutter. I can point out the crisscrossing rodent tracks on a macadam rail trail, and tell the story of the dog that jumped into the mud to chase a chipmunk. I still feel lucky for each little story that nature presents me with.

And really that's what tracking is about: reading the stories of nature. In the beach sand you can delight in the story of two seagulls fighting over a clam. In the winter snow you can follow the tale of a mink chasing a shrew right to its bitter end. And those stories spread out to include the entirety of human experience. Every fallen leaf is a track, every crack in a stone. The bones and skulls of men and animals are their last track, or nearly so, since at the molecular level we could track one life on and on, until the Sun's death turns all those scattered atoms into energy, and then, even then, we might follow those streams of light to the edge of the universe, and into the neighboring universe, and beyond.

Amy Nawrocki is the author of five poetry collections, including *Four Blue Eggs*, which was a finalist for the 2013 Homebound Publication Poetry Prize. Her most recent book, *Reconnaissance*, was released by Homebound in 2015. She teaches composition, literature and creative writing at the University of Bridgeport and lives in Hamden, Connecticut.

# Choosing Peregrine

## by Amy Nawrocki

But whether it was a bird of prey
Or prey of bird I could not say.
—Robert Francis

MY HUSBAND CALLS ME FROM UPSTAIRS. *Hurry. Quick. Look out the window. Do you see it?*

The front yard slopes toward the unseen road, about thirty feet from the house. The blacktop of our driveway and a low gray rock wall give way to a grove of trees, a blend of grey bark, brown earth, and the pale paper of lingering beech leaves. Thinned out in late autumn, the laurel trunks twist and spread their muted and monotone still-green foliage. A weathered stump and the lamp post are the only variables. Eric is pointing, directing my eyes, which see only the tessellation of space between laurel branches. There, behind the light, scan just to the right. The low branches. Do you see it? I have to find the movement with my eyes before I put the binoculars to work. He's told me by this time what I'm looking for—a peregrine falcon and its kill.

Neither of us has ever seen a falcon in the wild; we know they have been spotted near Sleeping Giant State Park, which isn't too far from our home, along the Blue Trail, across a few peaks. Our usual visitors are backyard feeder birds—woodpeckers, titmice, nuthatches, and juncos. Jays and crows come around and compete in summer months for the claim of noisiest and most imposing, but they're all talk. Red tailed hawks circle and we hear them call

or perch or swoop. They are familiar and welcome, and we've witnessed their kills more than once. They visit the southern end
of the road, where a solitary yearling uses poise and grandeur to
shake off the mild threat of young and inexperienced jays. This
peregrine, however, is not too much bigger than a crow or mourn-
ing dove, but unmistakable, once I finally find her with my assisted
gaze. We piece together the story. Something hit the window in
flight—fleeing or in pursuit—it was all so fast. Eric saw the falcon
take cover in the bushes. We watch the unfolding drama, passing
binoculars silently, as if we could be heard through the glass.

It's the junco's white belly that alerts me first. Shredded white
feathers—emptying as if from a torn pillow—scatter, not falling
to the ground but filling the space around the two birds. By the
time we've repositioned ourselves at the second floor window, the
peregrine has flown to a higher branch, a vantage point better for
our view, and more stable, perhaps, for the harder work of flaying
the junco's breast, a better angle for the scalpel beak, leverage for
talons. Through the binoculars, she is a giant, but the magnifica-
tion diminishes her effort. She could not have carried her prey
too much farther than the neighboring branch she decided on.
Downy, with elegant grey plumage, she wears speckles and delicate brown dashes on a whitish underbelly. I'm surprised by how
blue she is. The sky matches her with snow-worthy slate. At various angles, tawny cheeks and a black mask bob in steady motion,
shielding the claw-clutched prey, instinctually hiding what no one
else can have. Nothing else moves in the yard. She is at it for forty-
five minutes. I am at a loss for words. By the time it's over, all I
have is the conviction that *peregrine* is more melodic (and I think)
more accurate than *falcon*, and this is how she should be called.
That may be all the precision my retelling can muster.

I wonder about this as I sit down to my notebook. The camera has failed in such unforgivable ways, and memory is doomed to be insufficient. What else do I have? The worlds outside our windows should be shared worlds. I want to preserve the episode for my future self, to recount it at family gatherings, tell my friends through social media. I want to brag. But the nature we experience through others will always come through a filter. I take this to heart. "There is nothing in which people differ more than their powers of observation," wrote John S. Burroughs. As a nature lover, I cultivate my powers of observation. As a poet and teacher, I practice seeing and sharpen the senses by trying them out on paper. Like deciding to open the window or draw the shade, I deliberate on a point of view.

I told you about a junco, but it could have been a nuthatch, maybe the one I watched traipse down the oak this morning after insects which I haven't bothered to name. The woods are filled with unnamed critters, some visible for mere seconds at a time. Most never surface from earth cover or give up their camouflage or grow big enough to be noticed. Notice matters; spectacle speaks. The peregrine is singular; the everyday birds multiply and seem interchangeable. I may be able to describe any one of them from memory, if I could only be sure of its pedigree or be able to scan the table of contents of its daily migrations. As the peregrine's anonymity vanishes into a declaration of authority, the victim becomes just another white bellied meat source. That's one way of telling it. When I shift my vantage point, the quarry becomes small and delicate, slow, uncoordinated. A junco with its own story, its own beauty. Its black eyes pierce a cozy landscape of forests and food; a feed stop offers suet and kibble. A shadow passes; there is no escape. I hold my breath because I don't want to disturb the moment. I exhale, and I've already altered it.

Any snapshot is filtered by the viewer's eye and a lifetime of other sights. I do not intrude. Or do I? Our choice of words matters so much and we must consider them as we would territorial boundaries. If I say *surveillance*, do I imply deviance? If I chose *bird's eye view*, do you applaud my attention, or mock my sarcasm? If I say *hollow bones* rather than *banked blood*, which is accurate? When *staving off hunger* wins out over *lunch time*, the value of one sunflower *seed, one unlucky bird, goes* up like a sprinkler in a year of drought. The actions I describe can never be neutral, and you are always in my line of sight. Phrases like *habitat loss* echo through the woodlands like the tapping of beaks. *Survival of the fittest* signals the surrender of tree mites and dormant caterpillars. And juncos. As literate creatures, we hold much in our hands, the language of fight and of flight. The natural world—so vast and varied, so holy and violent—will one day disappear. We all will fade into the sepia print of the past. The endurance that nature teaches us is what we have to bear the loss. It may seem a small thing, but the way we catalog what we see can shape the extent of our preservation and shape our ability to heal and honor, celebrate and remember. It is an earned privilege—the naturalist as chronicler. If I say *watcher*, do you think *witness*? If I say prey, do you hear *prayer*?

*Peregrine*, from the Latin meaning "one from abroad." A wanderer, one who migrates. The peregrine stands 15 inches and can spread its wings three and a half feet. Peregrines mate for life. Both parents tend their young. The peregrine can catch prey in flight and reach speeds of 240 miles per hour. I choose to tell you this. Do you see it? She has pierced the windpipe with her talons and killed the bird instantly. She is hungry. She will eat its bones. She is beautiful. I try to capture her, but she flies away. She is both my words, and beyond them.

Andrew Jarvis is the author of *Sound Points* (Red Bird Press), *Ascent* (Finishing Line Press), and *The Strait* (Homebound Publications). His poems have appeared in *Appalachian Heritage, Evansville Review, Valparaiso Poetry Review, Tulane Review,* and many other magazines. He was a Finalist for the 2014 Homebound Publications Poetry Prize. He is also on the editorial board of Red Dashboard LLC. Andrew holds an M.A. in Writing (Poetry) from Johns Hopkins University.

# Northwest Blood

## A Poetic Offering by Andrew Jarvis

T HE COPPER RIVER IN ALASKA is famous for its Chinook, Sockeye, and Coho salmon. I have never been there. I rely on pictures and tales to experience its bounty. They are not artificial or doctored memories of the river. They are memories of people becoming one with nature, becoming the spirit of it as they work in water. There is so much life there, and it runs in color. I started thinking of the color red, and how it thrives in arguably the most fertile fishing waters in the world. Red is the color of blood, which is the essence of life. And as someone fishes in the river, they encounter red water, red salmon, and red roe. To experience the heart of it, I want to reach into the river and feel life pump through my hands. I want to experience how things survive and grow in a rugged, natural, and primal environment. This poem expresses that desire by creating a metaphor for human passion, growth, and the beautiful essence of life.

## River Life

Red runs like ink on a soft hand,
its fingers slicing mountain tops
and falling into colored skin.

This is a river of salmon
spawning water babies in roe,
spherical birth in fish scales.

We feel the surface, rolling
our fingers in radiant waves,
overflowing by water's edge.

As smooth as a ruby's façade,
we shine in their enlightenment,
the wet faces of river flow.

And we learn of life in color,
remembering those bloody hands
pulsing, glowing, thriving, in spawn.

"THE ARK" IS INSPIRED BY THE OZETTE MUDSLIDE near Neah Bay in Washington State. Ozette is the site of a Makah Indian village estimated to be more than 2,000 years old. The poem has a strong sense of place rooted within its ark, an ark which holds images of the history of the Makah people. The poem is realistic, as the tribe loses to the sea's power; however, it creates a strong sentiment in the end, as the tribe glows in history through its everlasting objects, the things they carried.

## The Ark

We will build an ocean
ark for our gatherings,
a ship for our arrows
and their delicate heads.

It will puncture the wave
of the tidal attack,
as if the beach molded
a great sand sword for us.

Fish hooks, harpoons, and rods,
the tools we have carried
and all of their catches,
a bank of fishing gems.

And then the land will end,
and water will swallow
our beach, our shore, our banks,
as if we baited it.

To eat us entire,
sink us in the daylight
and make everything night,
it will be ravenous.

And it will stay hungry
after we weld a craft
to crest the hungry sea
and glow within our pearls.

Walker Abel is retired director of Sierra Institute, an academic field school connected to UC Santa Cruz and Davis. He led environmental studies field programs for 27 years. His programs emphasized ecopsychology and nature literature and were taught entirely off-campus while on a series of backpacking trips through various wild areas of California. One of his greatest joys was watching each new group of students open over time to the transformative influence of wilderness immersion. Walker is also a poet, and he won the 2014 Poetry Prize from Homebound Publications with his book *The Uncallused Hand*. That book went on to be a Finalist in *Foreword Reviews'* 2014 Book of the Year Awards and to win Gold in the 2015 Nautilus Awards.

# The Confessions of
# a Land Squatter

## by Walker Abel

ROM DISTANCE, a squatting bobcat looks like no more than a bush or clump of grass. One fooled me today. I stood ground while my straining eyes wavered in their certainty, until finally at the end of patience I said, "no, it is a bush". Then with my first step, that "bush" leapt up and disappeared in cat smoothness. The squat is a position of readiness - the cat's low profile and perfect stillness camouflage a core of tensed aware-ness; its senses are open to the faintest triggers and thighs coil with waiting fire.

Similarly, a squatting man is hard to recognize. A casual gaze will pass him by. So, the word "squatter", is appropriate for one liv-ing secretly on land not his own. He squats in the thickets or on the walls of ravines, always second-guessing as to which place the owner would find most inaccessible. There he abides through sun and rain; the flow of day and night is like receding waves that bury his feet ever further in the earth.

This evening I sat on the slope of a hill and clacked two deer antlers together. The sound was dry and sharp, like stabs in the darkening body of the valley. Sure enough, it stirred the blood of a young buck, who strode from the forest in answer. He came up the slope with unrushed, elegant steps. When he suddenly caught my scent, he was gone in a series of flashing bounds, and I was left with the scorched image of his perfect poised body appearing and disappearing in airborne arches above the shrubs.

The secret of the buck's sprint is in the focused point of contact between hoof and earth. When he touches down for an instant, the merging is complete. Each cloven track is a mark of birth where he springs anew like lightning from the ground. The same is true with squatting—the essence is contained in the relationship between the bottom of the foot and the earth.

We are large animals, and especially in seasons of dryness, we are noisy when we move. Now there is certainly a time for vigorous hiking, and there are days when no other activity will suit me—I want to hike and scramble and clamber and crawl through so many miles of land and bush that by day's end, my body is worn light and I move with a contented ease. But such vigorous hiking and the attention it calls to oneself is not the way to blend in with the other lives on the land.

Downstream of my camp is a swamp created in some past drama of the earth—a huge slump on one wall of the canyon, damming the creek and leaving a vertical cliff of unstable soil above. I was there in the evening, sitting near the base of a redwood. The forest was very still—now and then, the gurgle of bubbles in the water or the inconspicuous sounds of birds. But suddenly, from the far end, there came the loud and raucous calling of a duck. Nothing to be alarmed about, except that the calling persisted. And it continued to persist beyond common expectation. I thought for a moment it might be a poacher, who could make a good imitation but was ignorant of when to stop. However, it was in fact a duck, and as it continued its noise, the other animals became disturbed and began to raise a hue and cry. First the jays sounded their complaint; then, three or four red squirrels appeared suddenly, stomping on limbs and convulsing their bodies with scolding. Even a dozen frogs chimed in, and the final authority, like a judge swinging the gavel, was the distant resonating call of a great horned owl.

As a land squatter, night contains my safest hours. In day, there is always the chance of being seen, while darkness surrounds me in certain sanctuary. Some nights I walk long into the darkness. In the meadows my bare feet can feel the dew thicken. Returning to camp through the trees and brush, it is pitch black, and I hold my arms protectively out front like long cat whiskers. The feet feel the way - through them and through indicators of sound and even fragrance, I guide my way back.

Almost every night, I like to wrap a blanket around my shoulders and sit before laying down to sleep. After I have been quiet a while, the wood rats begin to stir. It is just a faint rustling in the leaves as they go about their normal business. They do not forget me, for they know very well that I am here. But I smile and relax because in their unconcern it shows that I have been accepted as a denizen.

I view my stay on this land as an experiment in living. My purpose is to seek that which suits a person the way soaring on air currents suits a hawk. Like a Zen practitioner, I believe the essence is awareness, and the fact that I am technically in breach of the law is like the whacking stick of the master, keeping me alert to my surroundings and sensitive to my effects.

Like other units of experience, an experiment has a beginning and an end. I am now not more than half way into this, but there are times when I stand on the high hills and look over the sun-bathed land to the ocean, or when in full stride, I step into the scent of laurel blossoms, or other times stretched out relaxed on the limbs of an old oak, feeling like a large mass of moss, and in these occasions I am overwhelmed with the sense that I cannot love this moment enough. It is here, and I am here, and this is now; but I know that it will soon mysteriously, and undetectably, transform itself into the moment of parting, when the experiment must end.

Before the first rains of autumn—and today's is only the second of any consequence—the stalks of the meadow grasses were yellow and brittle and a deer walking could be heard a hundred yards off. In places, the soil was baked hard like old mud flats; in others, dry and crumbly, slipping away like sand under foot. But in the hottest days of dryness, when flaky fragments of stems and bark come in with every breath and stick to the back of the throat, urging thirst, even then, down in the depths of the ravines is discovered the secret movement of water. It is always akin to night down there, shadowy and cool, so steep are the walls and so thick is the canopy of trees and shrubs. The water is dark and slow; it slips snakelike underground and pops up again ten feet later. The flow—particularly the tiny flows before any creeks have merged—has the everlasting feel of the stars. Ferns and trees and drinking animals come and go, but the water moves. These are the most primeval places on the land. There is the sense that the fierce wildness retreats at the approach of civilization. Like a clam into its shell, it pulls down into these ravines, dragging behind it a shield of frustratingly dense growth, and all to protect its heart—the quiet flow of water.

I drink nothing but this water. If I go the six miles to town for provisions, I carry a canteen of it with me. Water is the blood of the earth and solvent of this land's qualities. When the water of my body is the water of this land, then I am a pool that has climbed from the ravine on two legs, moving about here and there, busy in my various actions, but always connected by secret sympathy to that dark flow from which I drink. And when I stand in the meadow under full moon, as much as I feel the liberating openness of that space, I feel also the deep pulse of the water as it first draws from the earth and begins its flow like night's breath among the rocks and sands and ferns, the moon pulling at it from far above.

With every new morning, as I wake and walk through the fading stars, I feel more and more invisible upon the land. On certain routes that I follow almost daily, my step is practiced, and I move along in a flowing choreography that makes partners of bushes, low limbs, fallen trees. In all movement, to engage the land in dance is a practice of oneness, for as Yeats asked, "Who can separate the dancer from the dance?"

I remember the day I met a bobcat and watched him bound off through the bushes. It struck me then that this land knows nothing of the so-called human owner who lives miles distant. He is an absentee, while each push of cat thigh and each ripple of cat fur was to the land as a wave is to the ocean. Title deeds are as pompous as dams on the Colorado—in the river's time, geologic in its vastness, those feats of engineering are ephemeral. The same with ownership of land—in the vast time of cycles, of seasons, years, and centuries—it is the land itself that chooses its residents.

Friends from town came to the woods for a visit today. We wandered the land as hawks would fly the air, granting to one another great leniency of space, freedom of thought and sense, yet ever circling back to moments of overlap and the winged rush of recognition.

We parted in early evening. In the moist depths of the forest, they were gone from sight while their voices still carried. That trailing sound of their murmured words pulled me like the sky-filled calling of geese, and I knew I would be returning soon. Solitude is an extreme condition. For days on end, the world can be as sharp and austere as a night landscape glimpsed in the bursting glare of a lightning bolt. Periodically, I need this intensity. Some part of me sleeps when I am out amongst people and only wakes again after the third or fourth day of being alone in the woods. It wakes slowly and cannot be rushed. I know it is here when I have the urge to go to the largest thickets and crawl down long tunnels, slither on my belly, wiggle between branches, until I am lost in that vast labyrinth. Suddenly, in some utterly private chamber, I stop. The scream of a hawk pierces from above, and as it ripples down my spine, I arch to the tingling and my fingers curl like claws into the dirt.

I took a farewell bath in the creek today. The water was cold; it stung my skin and breathing came in snatches. But I have learned with regard to cold-water bathing that once I pass beyond the initial resistance, I never regret doing it. The old law that one must give in order to receive is again proven true. After the sacrifice of my body to the cold, I lie on the banks and ride like spring from the south on the resurging wave of life and warmth.

As I walk from this four-month land of my solitude and return again to the world of employment and people, right at the border of the two, I come upon a huge redwood, cut by chain saw and as painfully stranded in the grass as a still-breathing whale. For a period of time, I find it hard to maintain my balance. But reluctantly, I come to admit that I am a denizen as much of where trees are lumber for houses as where trees are themselves. I gave myself to this land as one gives oneself to love, emulating the belongingness of bobcat, deer, hawk. And in parity, I received too, much as the land under touch of long and gentle rain seems to purr itself into well-being. Life is a succession of intimacies—some longer, some shorter. They all leave their impress in our mossy body of earth.

Audrey Henderson's writing is rooted in her early life on the edge of Edinburgh, Scotland, where the clash of city and country, ancient history and wrenching modern change began an enduring fascination with the interplay between the natural and the man-made environment. She lives in Boston and is active in the areas of literacy and environmental education. Her poetry has appeared widely in both Britain and the United States.

# Olmstead, 9/11 and Me

by Audrey Henderson

Friday 14 September, 2001

ODAY I AM RECKLESS, I seek risk. Before Tuesday I would not have done. But today I set off into the woods of Franklin Park unaccompanied, heedless of direction, bounding over rock outcrops, wastes of pocked stone. I find myself suddenly at the top of a 30 foot cliff. Safety has ceased to have meaning.

The terrain is erratic: boulders stand alone, boulders stick out of the ground, there is no soil or shallow soil. I range wantonly about this jagged landscape feeling jagged and bruised, feeling careless. Paths appear and I veer downwards, relishing the abrupt angle, the steep slope, with no map. There are no birds. Not no birds; a crow on a dead tree. The rain is heavy.

I dive into woods: sick hemlocks tagged for destruction. Fleshy mushrooms here, bunches of False Solomon's Seal, red and sometimes severed. It's good to be lost in wildness. My ravaged psyche seizes on the pitted and bloody, all the things of brokenness.

*Ouerhailet* is a Scottish word, a breathless word meaning overwhelmed. The poet Alexander Boyd used it in his love poem "Cupid and Venus." "From bank to bank, from wood to wood I run ourhailet by my feeble fantasie," I think of it as I run from bank to bank, not blinded and overwhelmed by love, but by too much death. I find charred places in the ground, several charred patches on the woodland floor. The air smells sharply of charcoal and beside one of the large black plumes lies a candle. A candle ignored by the fire it started. And this woodland is at the heart of the metropolis so there are singed bed sheets and bedclothes in damp heaps on the earth. There are buried socks. The seedy dangers I usually shun connect me to my desolation.

Yet I am surprised suddenly to realize that this abandon to the wild is soothing me. Here are striate bird's nests on a heap of woodchips. I stare down at the miniature fungi, shaped like egg-cups or bird's nests, full of tiny gray "eggs". I can hardly believe the delicacy and novelty of this arrangement, now on my knees, nose to the ground. Here are black puff-balls, bitter boletes, red russulas, pyrolas. Wherever I throw myself, the living land responds. Whichever un-promising dark grove I head towards embraces me. Some exchange is happening between skin and spore, between lung and air, between light and eye, an exchange of energies, a conversation between micro-biomes. I try to find an extreme environment and am held up within it by tiny and mysterious forces. They invite me to stop and look, they hook me with their microscopic energies. The woods are growing, slowing me down with their offering of gems, even as I try to hurl myself towards oblivion.

Maybe there is nothing in our own devastation that nature cannot counter. If you are exploding, I will explode, it says. If you are frozen, I am frozen too. Look! See this tree has grown for many years with a chain-link fence embedded it its heart. If nature can be extreme and harsh and cruel, it can also grow through whatever shards are embedded in us.

Monday 17 September 2001

THE SKY IS AN UNBEARABLE BLUE, as it was on 9/11. It leaves me feeling exposed, unprotected by the clouds whose mantle I trust. Today there is only utter infinity overhead. My head is heavy, as if all the absent clouds are stuffed behind my eyes. My legs are heavy and it's hot, the surprising heat of autumn afternoons that follow shivering mornings. I doubt my purpose. I expect too much, take too much for granted because of the marvels I have seen. I'm spoiled and petulant and want nature's wonders in capital letters and italics.

But there are only crickets, cabbage white butterflies, panicled hawkweed with a million orbs poised to shed seed to the wind. Two aggravated chipmunks fret actively. They have been hidden during the fecund summer, but now they are brazen and agitated. A small grey flycatcher sits on a leafless tree in the pear orchard; my guess is that it's a Least flycatcher, which is haunting open groves as it's supposed to according to Peterson's Guide. This is certainly an open grove, with wide sunny spaces between the trees, full of the *chirring* of crickets. It should be pleasant, yet I recoil from the alien sunshine. The numbness in me persists. I'm reluctant to chase a red dragonfly and grateful to get a second chance to examine it when it stays near me, resting on a faded bur-marigold. There are small black notches along its back, otherwise it is ruby red, like the red of the apples that lie on the ground. Other butterflies drift past, monarchs, more cabbage whites, orange skippers, yellow butterflies with black edges round their wings, yet I am hypnotized by the red fruits: the red fruits of bittersweet nightshade, the Mallus sergentii with hard berries, the dogwood berries and the apples, a red wastage of apples under the tree with too many crows.

By the end of the walk I'm humming an old fashioned Christmas carol about an apple tree and when I get home I look up the words:

*This fruit doth keep my soul to thrive*
*It keeps my dying faith alive*
*Which makes my soul in haste to be*
*With Jesus Christ the apple tree.*

They speak to this moment. My soul is not thriving, my faith is dying and yet it is also hastening to the apple trees. And here's the question: where is Jesus Christ right now? If only I could believe that he is somehow present in the apple tree, but this is an idea that the Episcopalian in me is not supposed to dwell on, old Christmas carols aside.

### Wednesday 19 September 2001

It is to Frederick Law Olmstead's enormous credit that I can feel panic at being lost in the woods within the Boston city limits. His paths defy my sense of direction and steer me away from my destination. This can sometimes be pleasant, at other times not.

I begin my tramp feeling desolation. I pick up garbage as a small contribution to nature and soon my bag is full. There are no bird sounds on the wastes of rock and dried grass. I meander in circles, finding a discarded T shirt in bright Check Casher yellow, advertising, yes, a Check Casher, size XL. The signs of distress multiply: blankets, clothes, water bottles. I finally decide that there is nothing here but the vestiges of human misery and distract myself with the exercise of identifying all the types of goldenrod and all the types of aster.

This problem with identification is an American one. Just as in Britain there are five basic sandwich types on any menu, the British flora is similarly streamlined, with one of everything, so that slight variations are mostly not a concern. Here in America there are seven pages in my flower guide devoted to goldenrod and probably as many for asters. I decide to take samples, so I'm plucking fat clumps of aster or small sprigs, when a wave of bird song surrounds me. The birds fill every tree and the air in between. Five tufted titmice on one branch, chickadees, nuthatches, Carolina wrens, a hairy woodpecker. I want not to be distracted by the locals so that I can concentrate on the migratory warblers flitting through the branches. A mighty yellow confusion of leaves and birds assails me and where do I turn first? My neck vertebrae crunch, my arms ache. Birds are everywhere and their spring plumage is gone. I can identify some—American redstarts, black and white warblers, parulas with their blue-grey backs and white wing bars, but what about the yellow bird with black rimmed under-parts? Is it too yellow to be a female orchard oriole? And is this a Philadelphia vireo? A yellow throated vireo? And what about this one—wing bars and streaks: a blackpoll warbler, and this one—sheer yellow below, sheer grey above, a Canada warbler?

I stand there with weeds poking out of my back-pack in a state of just-out-of-bed staleness, lank hair stuffed under a hat, staring up at the oaks, when a man comes round the corner singing loudly in a lunatic sort of way, with unselfconscious non-musicality. I look at him. He looks at me. We are alone in the woods, weighing each other up and which of us is more nuts? It's all so baffling, the differences slight, the range of distinguishing characteristics so very narrow.

Linda Flaherty Haltmaier is an award-winning poet and screenwriter. She was named a finalist for the Princemere Poetry Prize and her poems have appeared in journals and anthologies including *Canopic Jar, Mad Swirl, Poetry Breakfast,* and more. A Harvard graduate, Linda lives with her husband and daughter on Boston's North Shore—and strolls the beach in search of inspiration.

# A Muddy Resurrection

## A Poetic Offering by Linda Flaherty Haltmaier

I BREATHE A SIGH OF RELIEF at the first stirrings of spring. It's a slushy, muddy resurrection in New England as the sun asserts itself a bit longer each day, reviving and warming everything. In winter, I marvel at the survival skills of creatures, plants, and trees. I know that even with my out-sized human brain, I wouldn't last a day in the elements with just a fur coat and a can-do attitude.

I find myself ruminating on clogged snake holes, if the rabbits have found a cozy spot to ride out a Nor'easter, if the sparrows are chubby enough to make it another month. When they all re-emerge somehow, it feels like miracles are sprouting, creeping, and chirping everywhere I look.

## Up and Out

The birds sense it first,
the energy rising from the
damp earth,
the scratching of roots—
maples, field grass,
desiccated tiger lilies
ready for re-animation.
Pulpy fingerlings
shake off the chill,

annoying a beetle out
of his stupor—
to wobble his way
up through the soil
to the radiating warmth,
carapace glinting
like the hood of a '67 Mustang
in need of a good scrub—
his antennae alert for
the rumblings of life
erupting all around,
daring the birds
to stay preoccupied
with their flirting
and fluttering
in the glow
of spring's new day.

# 100 Inches and Counting

An inside cat,
that's what I've become,
yawning away the morning
as another storm blusters through.
I curl up at the window
to watch the politics
of goldfinches and blue jays
as they vie for prime spots
at the feeder,
the antagonist,
a furry acrobat
with plans to up-end the party and
shower seeds to the white ground.
Birds flit off to smaller trees
still mummified in snow,
trunks encased in icy wraps.
Only today, the buds on the
branch tips are changed—
dragon lady fingernails
point skyward in the swirl,
promising an end to this
muffled, inside existence.
Soon, winter will trickle
into storm drains
along with salty tales told
of the winter when snow banks
were higher than roof tops.

Mary Petiet is a reporter, writer and story teller. Her work is frequently inspired by her native Cape Cod, where she has covered the local farm beat for *Edible Cape Cod* for many years. She is a contributing author to the *Girl Guide Anthology, Jesus, Muhammad and the Goddess,* and has published a selection of essays and articles in a variety journals and magazines. A graduate of the University of St Andrews, Mary works as a reporter for the Bourne Enterprise newspaper. Her book *Minerva's Owls* is due out in April 2017, with Homebound Publications.

# Salt of Our Blood

## by Mary Petiet

Iwrote a poem about a sacred landscape when I was twelve. I never thought I'd share the poem, but it's the first thing that came to me when I imagined voices in a sacred landscape. The poem might have been longer, but this is what I remember of it.

> Marsh grass, withered and yellow
> The summer greens have recently mellowed.
>
> Beyond the grass the trees do flame,
> Brilliant shades only nature can claim.
>
> While in the creek the water laughs,
> Reminding us of summers past.

It's a kid poem, a kid attempt to express the sacredness of the marshy Cape Cod creek a short walk from my house. It's a profound place and I could hear its voices, but I lacked the vocabulary to fully understand them, much less express them. I spent hours of endless childhood at the creek with my yellow lab Magnolia.

Full disclosure: I still do. I walk it every morning. Back then, I'd sit on the remains of an old salt works blown out in a 1930's hurricane, overlooking the tidal creek connecting the fields to the south with the ocean to the north. Now I start each day there, walking with my pointer-lab mix Daisy.

This is my church.

A certain light infuses Cape Cod, especially at water's edge where we inhabit a thin arm jutting out into the Atlantic. Artists come here to paint the light, the result of a low tree canopy and the endless blue reflection of the surrounding sea. You can find the sibling of this light inhabiting Dutch art, flirting with the viewer from ornate museum frames, and running wildly off-canvas through the Dutch countryside. Light is energy in motion, and energy is the fuel of all life.

The marshy place where this light proliferates, where land meets sea against a backdrop of sky is a sacred place of beginnings and endings, alpha and omega, book-ended by the seasons, earth's knowing cycles. The tide comes in, the tide goes out. We receive, we give. There is stillness, and the odor of salt, the taste of salt, the recall of our own first floating in the maternal ocean, the recall of the salty soup from which all life emerged eons and eons ago. Our origins are here in the water, and they are preserved in the salt of our blood.

I am not the first to feel the sacredness of this place. The first native people here before me also felt it. They summered for countless generations on this north side beach along the endless tidal flats emerging twice daily where the creek gives out to the sea. The flats provide a banquet of shellfish which I harvest now as they once did. It seems they lived peacefully here, at least there is no evidence of strife. When a pilgrim boy went missing on an adventure, this is where they found him, safe with the Wampanoag.

Huge shell middens dot the landscape, mute testimony to ancient feasts, and who is to say Squanto, Massasoit, or a lost English boy did not throw any of the shells upon the pile? It would have taken many people to accumulate middens of this size, towering oyster and clam shells, implying a communal effort of joint harvesting and sharing. Implying the all-encompassing inclusion that furthers life instead of the narrow individualism that hinders it.

The first people are still here. A local farmer told me he found a series of ancient graves plowing the fields behind the beach. Bones and baskets ground up as he opened the earth, exposing the midden builders once more the Cape's light. He was working in isolation, hurrying to plant and harvest alone, so he told no one, and now crops grow over graves desecrated by the narrow individualism of the newcomers.

A wise woman also lived here once, exiled from the sea captain's village built well back from the ocean. Alone here she would have understood the sacredness of the place even as the first people died and the newcomers tried to harness it, own it, graze cattle and sheep upon it, and industrialize it for salt evaporation, clay extraction, and individual profit. Whispers of witchcraft, ostracization. I hope she embraced the freedom of the place as she existed wild in the dunes and the marshes, far beyond the pale of convention.

There is energy here. If ley lines conveying energy run through spots sacred to life, this is such a spot. I imagine a ley line running beneath my perch overlooking the creek. I felt the energy before I had the tools to articulate it. It inspired my clumsy poetry. The first people and the wise women are gone, we have no teachers to guide us, but still we feel the energy's pull, life's assertion.

The marshy place where land meets sea is also sometimes edged with death and decay. Summer fades to fall, to winter, and we fade from vital to pale imitations of our youthful selves. Lush green fades to yellow and then to brown, the storm clouds gather and the smell of salt becomes a rank breath from the grave. Life seems suspended, sea water freezes in glacial patterns and dead schoolies and eider duck wash up upon the shore. The sweet salty breath of life is balanced by the cold winds of winter, in an endless cycle, sustained by the deep underlying energy that powers all.

I walked my dog down the beach in the cold late fall to the spot of my perch overlooking the creek as my sister faced dangerous surgery to remove a cancerous kidney. The air felt alive, stopping me short. There was something here to remember, something unplanned coming through.

I leaned to the east, and thought life. The sun was rising and I felt the touch of its light through the chill air. I leaned to the west, and thought death, of endings and sunsets, the dark descending. I turned to the south and imagined the breezes of summer, the scent of roses from the fields and life at its healthy prime. I leaned to the north and felt the cold coming down from arctic places, and thought of endings and the grave.

This is sacred space. This is my church. As the energy took me, I asked it to save my sister, that her winter might end again in spring, that she might receive the life energy coursing through me, and be whole once more. I opened my arms wide and sent it to her.

Gary Whited is a poet, philosopher and psychotherapist. Before developing a private practice in psychotherapy, he taught philosophy at The University of Montana, The University of Texas, and at Emerson College in Boston. He presents workshops in the U. S., Europe and Russia, which focus on the practice of deep listening as a vehicle for change and for healing. His book of poems titled, *Having Listened*, was selected as the winner of the 2013 Homebound Publications Poetry Contest, and in 2014, his book received a Benjamin Franklin Book Award. *Having Listened* offers a collection of poems that speak from the confluence of a childhood on the prairie remembered and an encounter with the haunting voice of Parmenides echoing across 2500 years. He is currently working on a new translation of the entire poem of Parmenides and a second poetry manuscript. He lives in Boston, is married and has a grown daughter and son and three grandchildren.

www.garylwhited.com

# Listening to Our Listening

## by Gary Whited

L AST SUMMER I SAT ON TOP OF HURRICANE POINT overlooking Silver Lake in central New Hampshire. Wind sounded through scant trees on the steep little hill mingled with the hum of a distant motorboat, then two of them. Their wake slapped against the shore at the foot of the hill. I heard its splash again and again until it went silent. Someplace deep in memory I heard the sound of wind on the prairie, how different it was from the wind here among trees and over water.

For every one of us there is a story to our listening. It started in some particular place, then traveled and evolved from that place and time to now. If we listen for it, we can hear the story of our own listening, and each of our stories differs from all others. Consider right now as you read this where your story began.

A storm seemed to be gathering over Silver Lake. I noticed the darkening air and the smell of rain. For a while the wind stopped, no boats passed by, yet my ears and my entire body kept listening. I thought to myself, does it ever stop? I've heard that hearing is the last sense to go when someone is dying. Maybe our listening keeps on going as near to the end as it can get, right out to the edge of breath. Maybe it dares to approach anything, any edge, any precipice. When places inside me get frightened, or happy, or sad at what I hear, listening goes on through it all, a vehicle for travel all around me and inside me.

As I look back over my life, all the way to its beginning, I recognize that my listening was taking its earliest shape by what surrounded me in that place of prairie, its many voices of wind from quiet breeze to fierce gust, the voices of all the creatures that lived there and became my first guides. As a boy walking the pastures this is what I heard:

## Night Hawk's Path

It happened the first time
on the dirt cow path
when I walked
behind the milk cow,
evening chore-time light
gliding across Shadwell creek
now shadowed for the night.
When I stood still,
that hum
no one ever talked about, coming
from the earth, moved
up my legs
into my hips, turning
this body into sound.
Light flared yellow,
gathered around haystacks,
fenceposts,
the cow and me.

Writing that poem opened my listening to the prairie again. Remembering earth's hum coming into my body as these lines came to me became its own kind of listening, bringing this hum back to me a second time as a gift.

The particular place on this planet that, for each of us, first shaped our listening stands amidst this larger place we inhabit together called cosmos by the ancients. Not only our planet earth, but all the rest of the solar system, our galaxy, and everything beyond, whatever that is, both what we know and what we don't know of it surrounds us, touches us on every side, shapes us and our listening in uncountable ways. Everything out there is coming at us, and everything out there offers its signal whether or not we have a name for it. I am compelled to imagine that a larger "hum" than even that of planet earth alone comes toward us always and in each moment.

Reflecting on my experiences on the prairie, where things and people came to me in tactile and visceral ways, I like to think that listening is close to touch in its essential nature. It invites into us whatever presses itself toward us on whatever organ of reception we offer. It can be our ears we offer to the words someone speaks, so we hear their story. It can be the heart we offer to the outpouring of another's grief as we hear of their loss. It can be the hand we offer to someone's reach for help, our mind that receives the imprint of another's idea, or the entire body that receives the invitation of a lover.

Though we think of listening most often as the experience of sound landing in our auditory capacity to hear, at its essence listening is receptivity, and we receive in many ways. That the hearing-impaired find other vehicles for listening than the auditory system testifies to this.

*        *        *

L ISTENING HAPPENS IN THE CALL and response between those who participate in it and co-create it. A third "something" emerges when listening blossoms, and it carries the one calling and the one responding along a path they travel, trading call and response back and forth. When it ignites and is most alive, it is a kind of fire, its flames reaching for anything that offers something to be heard, and everything offers something.

There is nothing to do. Listening is the most natural response we offer to whatever being or creature in the cosmos calls to us in its way. The rattlesnake calls with its rattles ripping through the silence around its long body coiled in the bush when we walk past. We respond with our startle, our fear, our moving out of harm's way. The river calls to us with its murmur. We respond with our ears taking it in, and with our being moved by its gentle yet fervent whisper along its banks. Another person calls to us with her request for the salt shaker, for a helping hand, for an ear to hear her story. We respond with our ears, our hands, bellies and hearts, our touch and our willingness to be touched.

*   *   *

WHEN OUR LISTENING TRULY OPENS, it will almost surely carry us to something we don't yet know. Believing we know what's coming, we are less open. If we embrace not knowing, we might become aware of a silence inside, an absence of preconceptions. Not "listening for" what we already think we know, we might come into a stillness where we experience what Heraclitus, the ancient Greek philosopher, urges us toward when he says, "If you don't expect the unexpected, you won't find it."

*   *   *

BUT WHAT ABOUT THE TIMES WHEN OUR LISTENING FAILS? When we fail to hear another, or we turn away from what the

other is saying, what is happening then? What is missing? And
what about all this time when we hear the news of our planet
being destroyed by our consuming habits? How can we truly be
listening yet still cascading toward environmental devastation? If
it is so natural and easily opened to what is around us, how come
it seems to close or be distorted at times?

I venture this. Our listening gets shaped in ways that constrain
it, that warp it around a particular belief, an expectation, an agenda, or an old wounded place inside. When this happens listening
becomes protective. It closes at the places where some part of us
is trying to steer away from an unwanted feeling or thought. This
happens both on an individual and a collective level. Our culture,
our patriotism, our religious or scientific orientation, political per-
suasion, personal agendas, historical traumas, all of these shape
and constrain our listening. We see this in the strife of the world
today, in the war torn Middle East or Ukraine, in the fight for
environmental sanity, anyplace where intense and polarized activity erupts in the absence of open and responsive listening.

*        *        *

It CAN BE MORE SUBTLE THAN THESE EXAMPLES. Even our
agenda to help someone can constrain our listening, turn it
into an instrument we are trying to wield rather than an open ves-
sel ready to receive another's call. I practice psychotherapy and at
times my desire to help my clients does affect how I listen. When
I take myself to be an instrument of healing, I'm less a healer. I've
learned that if there is anything to do to enhance my listening,
it is to listen with compassion and curiosity to those very places
where I am vulnerable and protective and where some door might
be ready to open.

# In this Body

There are rooms
that close their doors.
Years pass
and a breeze moves through.
Maybe it was the look of that man
with red hair and heavy hands,
or the woman crossing the street
with the soft fingers
and far away stare.
A door blows open slightly,
the hinges barely agree.
Behind that door
there's a small child
who wants you
to call him by name.

In my work as a psychotherapist my first task as I enter into relationships with clients is to listen ongoingly to my own listening.
My next task is to guide clients toward listening to theirs, to help
them discover where it might be blocked yet ready to open, ready
to receive the call from a scared or lonely part of them who wants
to know that someone is there, finally, and listening.

I try to remember as I sit down to each session that I could
approach it as I would a poem I've not heard before, and that I
want to hear the poem in its own terms, to be open to its voice and
what it might reveal to me. When my listening as therapist opens
in this way, I feel myself leaning in more, noticing subtle changes

in the tone, the gaze, the posture; tracking this person's story as it unfolds through voice and body. A deepening curiosity guides me toward what is ready to show itself.

When a client responds to the invitation, there is and there is not a therapist and a client. While I might be the guide at times, what really happens is two people listen to each other, bear witness each to the other. It is a profound event when it happens, and the two of us do not leave the same as we entered. Something has called us toward that boundary where our knowing borders our not knowing, opens us to the unexpected in the face of which we are likely to feel vulnerable, excited or both. If we keep listening there, places in us begin to appear that haven't been heard maybe ever, and what they reveal guides us further along the way. This is also where, if ever we do, we're likely to receive some kind of guidance from sources for which we don't have names, at least not yet.

This applies beyond the psychotherapy dialogue, to countries at peace or at war, to parents and children, to relationships of all kinds, and to all of us together in our struggle to save our natural environment. Let us listen to each other as well as to what the river says, what the tree says, the sky and the field, all of it.

In any dialogue witnessing grows out of this listening to our listening. This might be the most profound agent of change we have as humans who speak, who grieve, who weep and laugh, who offer to travel with another to yet unknown places. A few lines of a poem from Rumi speak to this:

> *Talking can be sweet. A field can bloom in your*
> *Eyes when sharing words with the right person....*
> *Find some ears that love the touch of your*
> *Sounds, and you theirs.*

This is what we have to offer one another, nothing more and nothing less. Our authentic and open listening reveals more of who we essentially are, each of us to ourselves and to one another. It is a profound offering, it is fierce and it asks everything of us.

Jason Kirkey is an author, ecologist, and the founder of Hiraeth Press. He grew up in the Ipswich River-North Atlantic Coast watershed of Massachusetts. Inspired by the landscapes in which he has lived—the temperate forests and old mountains of New England and the Eastern Piedmont, the red rocks and high desert of Colorado, Irish hills and sea—his work is permeated with an ecological sensibility. Whether poetry or prose, Jason's words strive towards consonance with the ecosystem. He has written four volumes of poetry, including *Estuaries* and a nonfiction book, *The Salmon in the Spring: The Ecology of Celtic Spirituality*. Jason is working on his second nonfiction book, *The Riverway: Field Notes for a Contemplative Ecology*. He now lives near Boston.

# The Wind in the Pines
## *Poetry and the Language of the Earth*
### by Jason Kirkey

MINNOWS SCATTER LIKE STARLINGS FROM A FIELD as I step into the water. I wade out carefully over stones worn smooth and slippery, roll up my pant legs and walk until I am up to my calves in the pond. I stop and stand as still as the heron stands. The minnows eventually return to investigate my feet. The wind gusts in successive waves, blowing through the white pine needles that hang above my head, bending the reeds and grasses, carving ripples in the surface of the otherwise still water. I stand in the water for a while, listening, watching, and eventually writing down a few words that would later become a poem. The air itself is silent, but it shakes the pines, bends the reeds, ripples and waves the water—it speaks through the world, plays it as music: a wild quartet.

In a technical sense, language is built up of phonemes and morphemes, of syllables, words, and sentences. Less technically, language can be considered a system of communicating or sharing meaning. Everything speaks if you know how to listen. The soughing of pine branches is a manner of speech. More than ordinary speech, it is poetry. There is poetry in clouds brushing the granite and pine face of a mountain, in the infinitesimally slow growth of hemlock and Douglas fir, in the lightning-strike-on water of a heron's beak. There is a disarming simplicity to these things that strips us down, even if only for a moment, to that same simplicity of being.

"Poetry is the resonance of being," writes Robert Bringhurst. Poetry is the sound of things echoing through their own emptiness into the world. He goes on to say, "It is the resonant silence you hear, and the resonant silence you make in return, when you get the poem and the poem gets you. When you really *see what it means*, what you see is nothing, and the nothing sings a song— one you may want to say you feel instead of hear."[1] What resounds is the is-ness of things. By is-ness I mean what Chinese philosophy calls *ziran,* which translates to "that which is so of itself." That which is so of itself effortlessly expresses its is-ness, its essential nature. Like a lightning strike on a mountain, *ziran* is an eruption of meaning into form and being.

The wind in the pines is this sort of poetry. Nothing about this poetry is separate from the poetry we humans make. Walt Whitman's *Leaves of Grass* is poetry, of course. It is the sound that Walt Whitman makes when the wind blows through him. But an actual leaf of grass is poetry too. All resound through silence with meaning and being. That is the meaning of language that has been cut loose from civilized life and linguistic theory, language that is allowed to return to the wild from where it originally came. All language is a subset of the poetry of flesh, leaf, wind, tooth, and stone.

Language moves through the whole web of interrelationships that constitute ecosystems. Typically, we think of these webs as food webs: who is eating whom? But just as tooth and tongue are the pathways that nutrients take from one organism into another, language is the pathway that meaning takes. The earth speaks through the sound of water over river rocks, the loping gait of a wolf as it stalks an elk, the still, waiting beak of a heron, the pat-

---

1 Bringhurst, Robert. *The Tree of Meaning: Language, Mind, and Ecology.* Berkeley: Counterpoint Press, 2008. 309

ter of rain on leaves. Such speech is food in the ecology of mind.

As much as we eat each other's flesh, we also consume each other's meaning—the poetry of things sustains us aesthetically. In its classical sense, the word aesthetic means to sense or perceive, coming to us from German through the Greek words *aisthetikos* and *aisthanesthia*. It is related in this way to our word of opposite meaning, anesthesia. The poetry of things enlivens us and brings us into our senses.

Conservationist Aldo Leopold's land ethic states very simply that, "A thing is right when it tends to preserve the integrity, stability, and beauty of the biotic community. It is wrong when it tends otherwise."[2] Why beauty? Beauty is the nutrient of poetry. Beauty is what engages the ecology of our bodies and minds, connects us into consonance with the ecology of the earth. It nourishes us aesthetically, emotionally, spiritually the same way food nourishes us physically.

In ancient Greek philosophy, beauty was identified with virtue and "the good." The beautiful is the aesthetic, and so to make sense of Leopold—indeed, to make sense of ecology—we have to widen the scope of what we might consider beautiful. The aesthetic need not be pretty or pleasing. The scent of a grizzly bear, musky and fecal, is not particularly pleasing, but it most definitely brings you sharply back to your senses.

From the comfort of our homes or around the glow of the fire, it is easy to associate the aesthetic with a sense of awe for the natural world or the feeling of kinship and belonging to it, but having aesthetic relationships in the wilderness can be a matter of life or death. Whether you're a human or an elk, a moment of lapsed attention can get you killed. The ecological community

---

2 Leopold, Aldo (1953). *A Sand County Almanac with Essays on Conservation from Round River.* New York: Ballantine Books, 1966. 262

depends on the web of interrelationships to stay sensually awake, just as it depends on that same web for its physical nourishment. The deeper, more spiritual feelings of awe and of belonging to the earth come naturally out of this, because such relationships require that we situate and identify ourselves within the larger ecology of things.

There are plenty of things in nature that are not pretty or beautiful to our "civilized"[3] sensibilities but which are nonetheless essential to the biotic community. No one is giving their sweetheart a bouquet of slime molds and a box of dung beetles, certainly. Yet fungus, mold, insects, bacteria, decomposition, and decay are all essential to the functioning of ecological communities. The sort of beauty I am speaking of runs deeper than prettiness. As poet Fredrick Turner wrote, "Beauty...is the highest integrative level of understanding and the most comprehensive capacity for effective action. It enables us to go with, rather than against, the deepest tendency or theme of the universe."[4] Such is the role of poetry in the food web, to integrate us into the deepest tendencies of the earth: the *dào*.

When I was a graduate student in ecology, I had many conversations with my adviser about learning to see the world differently, to learn to observe as an ecologist. This was the single most important component of my studies—far more crucial than learning research design or how to assess peer-reviewed literature. Those are skills, but how we perceive the world is part of who we are in the deepest strata of our being. Beauty must be tracked in the same way a bear can be tracked through the mud, or the browsing habits of elk can be read over multiple years by observing the

---

3 Here I mean civilized in its sense of being rooted in the life of the city, rather than the wilderness.

4 Turner, Frederick. *Rebirth of Value: Meditations on Beauty, Ecology, Religion, and Education*. New York: State University of New York Press, 1991. 13

patterns of growth and clipped stems. The ability to observe and read these signs changes how one perceives the biota of a place—observer included—as embedded in the landscape.

Beauty is information that travels along the web of ecological relationships in the same way energy and nutrients travel through a food web. A paw print in the mud or a nibbled stem is a *difference* in the landscape. Every "word" spoken by the ecosystem, every utterance of poetry—a ripple on the lake, the flash of tail by a fleeing deer, the croak of frogs—is a difference amongst the myriad relationships, living or non-living, that constitutes an ecological community. We have to learn to read the poetry of ecosystems the same way one learns to reads tracks and signs across a landscape—and to let it reshape and nourish our minds the way food nourishes and shapes our bodies. That is how we might come into consonance with the aesthetic of wildness, into consonance with the dào. That is what it means to eat beauty, to eat meaning, to eat poetry.

The elk at the forest edge resound with poetry, and their poetry transforms the landscape through their being, by shaping the structure of plant communities through their patterns of browsing, or by becoming food for carnivores. Without the elk, without the wolf, without the aspen, the "words" of the ecosystem's poem change, for better or worse. This language is a matter of life and death, a matter of ecosystem structure, and resilience.

We can study empirically how the poetry of wolves, beavers, termites, and maple trees affect and transform their ecological communities. But how does our own poetry—decaying into the soil, floating in the air like seeds, or washing away in the rain—feed the ecology into which we are embedded? This is a question at the heart of our humanity. We are what we eat, and out here everyone is eating flesh and poetry. Every member of the ecological community must eat this flesh of meaning. If we wish to be a part of this community, we must eat it too. So it is that the wildness of our language matters—not our words, but the poetry of our being that is spoken by the winds of this earth blowing through us.

Our voices as of late have become dissonant with the wild. This has changed the web of trophic poetry, and in turn changed the landscape. We have de-wilded the land through fragmentation, habitat conversion, and the extirpation of species. It is the imperative of our times to rewild. This task cannot solely be a matter of landscape management and conservation action. It must also be a matter of poetry, of relearning the wild poems at the heart of our humanity, of relearning to speak in consonance with the vernacular of mountains and rivers. Then we might make a beautiful meal of ourselves to the earth and feed the wild as the wild keeps on feeding us.

## HOMEBOUND PUBLICATIONS
*Ensuring that the mainstream isn't the only stream.*

At Homebound Publications, we publish books written by independent voices for independent minds. Our books focus on a return to simplicity and balance, connection to the earth and each other, and the search for meaning and authenticity. Founded in 2011, Homebound Publications is one of the rising independent publishers in the country. Collectively through our imprints, we publish between fifteen to twenty offerings each year. Our authors have received dozens of awards, including: Foreword Review Book of the Year, Nautilus Book Award, Benjamin Franklin Book Awards, and Saltire Literary Awards. Highly-respected among bookstores, readers and authors alike, Homebound Publications has a proven devotion to quality, originality and integrity.

We are a small press with big ideas. As an independent publisher we strive to ensure that the mainstream is not the only stream. It is our intention at Homebound Publications to preserve contemplative storytelling. We publish full-length introspective works of creative non-fiction as well as essay collections, travel writing, poetry, and novels. In all our titles, our intention is to introduce new perspectives that will directly aid humankind in the trials we face at present as a global village.

WWW.HOMEBOUNDPUBLICATIONS.COM

Lightning Source UK Ltd.
Milton Keynes UK
UKOW02f1216271116
288651UK00002B/11/P